PAUL HUSON

How to Test and Develop Your ESP

+ □ ☆ ○ 〜

MADISON BOOKS
Lanham • New York • Oxford

Standard ESP Cards reproduced by permission of Dr. J. B. Rhine

First Madison Books edition 2001

This Madison Books paperback edition of *How to Test and Develop Your ESP* is an unabridged republication of the edition first published in Briarcliff Manor, New York, in 1975, with the exception of five textual emendations and the deletion of chapter twelve ("Studying Parapsychology") and an appendix. It is reprinted by arrangement with the author.

Designed by Ed Kaplin

Published by Madison Books
4720 Boston Way
Lanham, Maryland 20706

12 Hid's Copse Road
Cumnor Hill, Oxford OX2 9JJ, England

Distributed by National Book Network

Library of Congress Cataloging-in-Publication Data

Huson, Paul.
    How to test and develop your ESP / Paul Huson.
      p. cm.
    Originally published: New York : Stein and Day, 1975.
    Includes bibliographical references and index.
    ISBN 1-56833-183-5 (pbk. : alk. paper)
    1. Parapsychology. I. Title.
BF1031 .H869 2001
133.8—dc21   00-068713

♾™ The paper used in this publication meets the minimum requirements of American National Standard for Information Sciences—Permanence of Paper for Printed Library Materials, ANSI/NISO Z39.48–1992.
Manufactured in the United States of America.

CONTENTS

How to Test and Develop Your ESP

I believe that the so-called "normal man" is a mere extract from the potentially realizable individual whom he represents, and that we all have reservoirs of life to draw upon, of which we do not dream. The practical problem is "how to get at them."
—WILLIAM JAMES (in a letter to W. Lutoslawski, May 6, 1906)

ONE

The Reality of ESP

The purpose of this book is to help you develop and experience your own faculty of extrasensory perception—to act as a guide to your adventures in the intriguing field of ESP.

That you *do* possess ESP is something you will soon experience for yourself, if you have not already done so. It is an ability we all share to some degree. It can take many forms: mind-to-mind communication, inexplicable premonitions of coming events, or a baffling ability to influence material events with your mind. Many of these things you may have read about but never witnessed or experienced for yourself. I hope that through this book you will.

The faculty responsible for all these exciting manifestations lies deep within each and every one of us, and like all our other capacities it can be exercised and developed. To what extent we develop it, and in what direction, depends on our individual aptitudes and on how much time we are willing to invest.

This book is a nontechnical personal record of ten years of experiments in developing and testing my own ESP. Most of the techniques included are those that I myself have found workable and productive. As you will see, they require persistence and knack rather than effort and brainwork—rather like learning to use chopsticks or ride a bicycle. *Why* they work is for the parapsychologist to find out. And in practical terms, the "usefulness" of the psychic faculty they uncover is moot as yet. ESP is bigger than we are, and trying to direct it toward highly specific goals often seems like the tail trying to wag the dog! (As you will see, one way we detect ESP is when the experimenter makes more wrong guesses than the law of averages would allow!) Our theoretical knowledge of it is still very limited, chiefly on account of a lack of a generally accepted overall theory, and our practical knowledge is even more so. We are still at the rule-of-thumb level, comparable to the ancient knowledge that rubbing amber with a silk cloth produces static electricity. We see the result, but we don't really know why it happens.

Fortunately, you don't have to understand ESP in order to experience it. You may not be able to levitate tables (most of us can't), but if you are anything like me, discovering that you can heal someone's headache by ESP or become aware of other people's unvoiced thoughts or sense what is inside sealed envelopes *is* a great adventure. It also tends to alter your point of view on life in a very special way, as you may shortly find out for yourself.

Because it is fairly typical of the kind of discovery you can expect to make about your own powers, let me tell you of an experience I had at a lecture in New York.

"If you're going to take parapsychology seriously," Dr. Osis had said in his gentle Finnish accent, "then you should know how it feels to take one of Rhine's card-guessing tests."

Karlis Osis is a former pupil of J. B. Rhine, the man considered by many to be the father of modern parapsychology. Osis himself is director of research for the American Society for Psychical Research, one of the more important scientific research groups in the psychic research field today.

A groan went up from the assembled ASPR members, many of them students like myself. We all knew what lay ahead. Dr. Rhine's tests had helped gain scientific credence for the phenomena of ESP back in the 1930's and 1940's. They are of great interest to the researcher but become increasingly boring to the subject of the experiment—stultifying if pursued to any great length, which unfortunately is the only way one can obtain statistically significant results from them. As psychics Eileen Garrett and Basil Shackleton once complained, there is nothing like forced-choice tests (as they are now called) for reducing an ESP sensitive buzzing with impressions to a block of insentient wood. The one redeeming feature of the test is Rhine's famous deck of cards designed especially to test ESP: five sets of decorative, cabalistic-looking symbols—star, circle, square, cross, wavy lines—which lend a touch of imagination to a game that quickly grows dull.

But Dr. Osis insisted, so we dutifully wrote in our special ESP test forms the symbols of the cards we felt were being turned up by someone in another room. I was not sure what I was supposed to do. The best I could think of was to keep telling myself enthusiastically that I would get a good score.

Nobody was more excited than I when I did. Out of twenty-five calls I had guessed ten correctly. That may not seem very impressive to you, but to me it sounded like a lot, although my excitement dampened somewhat after Dr. Osis explained the scoring method. Out of twenty-five calls using a deck of five sets of five symbols, the chance expectation was five correct guesses. In plain English, after discounting your first five hits, you start winning. So I had chalked up five ESP hits? Maybe, said Dr. Osis, maybe not. In an abbreviated test like this, you couldn't tell. Statistics need quantity to be meaningful, and this was merely a demonstration run.

Notwithstanding the disclaimer, however, he headed in my direction when the meeting broke up. One of the things you find out about parapsychologists is that they tend to keep an eye open for potentially high-scoring ESP subjects.

So, several days later I found myself sitting in Dr. Osis's New York office with a pad of blank paper before me, a pencil in my hand and my eyes screwed shut as I gazed into inner space. Two rooms away Dr. Osis opened the first of three previously prepared envelopes, scrutinizing the picture it contained and, I presume, endeavoring to beam his impressions of it in my direction.

"You can try closing your eyes and watching the pictures that form behind your eyelids," he had suggested earlier. I stared. Finally, out of the murk, shapes did begin to emerge. I seized on one gratefully. A black square object, was it? The afterimage of my pad of paper perhaps? I couldn't be sure. I got it in my head that it was a black swimming pool—rather an odd thing, when you come to think about it. I started to sketch it.

When I signified completion of my first drawing, Dr. Osis opened the second envelope. On closing my eyes I saw a spiny blob with a smaller blob attached to it. Ah, a cactus, I thought. I scribbled a sketch of my impression. When I shut my eyes to receive the third and last telepathic volley, I observed with irritation that the cactus shape was still there behind my eyelids. I waited for it to go away, but it didn't. It melted somewhat and finally turned into a statue of some sort. My first thought was Chinese soapstone. No, I decided, it was more like a Madonna and Child statue. I drew a Madonna and Child.

"Which target pictures do you think correspond to which of your calls?" asked a smiling Dr. Osis after he checked the results.

I stared at the targets.

Envelope number one had contained a magazine clipping of a grim scene all too familiar to us then—the Kennedys' black limousine at Dallas, foreshortened and therefore roughly rectangular. I had drawn a dark square, but hardly a limousine. In any case it was probably only a complementary retinal afterimage of the yellow pad itself. But why interpret it as a black swimming pool?

Dr. Osis silently slid the contents of envelope number two toward me. It was a coffee ad. Again, it had been clipped from a magazine. A small girl perched on the rim of a giant cup of coffee, apparently about to take a dive into its black depths. A black swimming pool? That was one way of describing it. Nowhere, however, was there any suggestion of a cactus, or cactuslike, shape.

Envelope number three turned out to be a direct hit. It also supplied the answer to the cactus riddle. It contained a photo of my Madonna and Child statue, a colorful Mexican altarpiece surrounded by a massive aureole of spiny gold rays. I recognized the aureole as my "cactus" immediately. Somehow, like the idea of the black swimming pool, the shape of the aureole had leaked back and contaminated my previous impression.

A string of coincidences?

For me, that stretches the meaning of the word too far. Like many people, I have had experiences that seemed telepathic, even if not provably so. But here was a deliberate and careful attempt to exercise ESP that turned up provocatively accurate results, to say the least.

My experience set me thinking. How had I done it? Could anyone do it? What else, what other strange psychic things could one do? And more especially, what do they portend? How many of us, I wonder, have ever considered what it would be like really to communicate, to know and feel the very thoughts and emotions as they pass through another person's mind? Or how would our anxieties about human frailty change if we found we could teach ourselves to recharge our depleted physical energies by mental means? How, too, would our feelings of overwhelming unimportance change if we discovered our minds had an inborn power to foresee the future, a power capable of viewing the overall pattern of events and our own unique place in it? These are only a few of the avenues explored by today's psychic researcher.

Perhaps it is because of these extraordinary prospects that some of the greatest names in science—more than a few of them Nobel prize winners—have taken an active interest in the subject: J. J. Thomson, the discoverer of the electron, Lord Rayleigh, discoverer of argon, Pierre and Marie Curie, discoverers of radium, and Albert Einstein, to name just a few of the physicists.

Pioneering psychologists Carl Gustav Jung, Sigmund Freud and William James were all deeply concerned with psychic phenomena.

Today, Soviet science has an edge on the West in that, while insisting on its customary determinist approach and deploring sensational accounts of psychic miracles, it now urges the serious investigation of the field. And about time. Psychic research has been conducted for over one hundred years now, and parapsychology for over sixty. The recent acceptance of parapsychology—the psychological approach to psychic phenomena —as a legitimate branch of science by the American Association for the Advancement of Science is a great milestone in its history in the West. Its struggle for recognition here has been long and hard, and even today, in an academic world teeming with grants and endowments, psychic research is still pitifully short of funds. As an academic course it is usually an adjunct to another —generally psychology, sometimes philosophy, rarely physics. It still has to contend with deeply entrenched suspicion and hostility in many scientific circles. These attitudes, one can only conclude, stem from an ignorance of the subject compounded by a fearful reluctance to associate one's name with something long lumped together on library shelves with flat-earth theories and fortune-telling. Where the evidence of parapsychologists is examined and accepted, the current "uselessness" of the phenomena—useless as the glow of radium or the electric power of amber, maybe?—is then given as a reason for parsimony, presumably because we cannot yet eat it or drop it on our enemy's head.

Perhaps we are being too charitable. The most cogent reason may well be an almost religious reluctance to confront the threat that psychic phenomena are seen by some to pose to textbook physics.

Back in the 1920's Dr. Rhine adopted the French psychic researcher's term *parapsychology*, partly as a concession to hostile reactions from the Duke University Psychology Department, partly to separate his study from the ectoplasm-shrouded spiritualism of the day. Since then, many, including Rhine himself, have come to believe that the phenomena not only transcend the principles of physics but can only be understood from a totally new metaphysical standpoint unrecognized by science.

Not all psychic researchers, however, feel this way. The word *parapsychologist* carries the built-in implication that the roots of the phenomena lie in psychological causes. Rhine might just as well have called the new science paraphysics, however, as some parapsychologists are doing today, for its physical implications are as significant as its psychological ones. Despite the fact that the phenomenon of precognition—the foreknowledge of future events—still causes intellectual heartburn among theorists, they feel the explanation of psychic phenomena will ultimately fall within the domain of physics, not metaphysics. In the capricious elusiveness of psychic powers—their often-observed reluctance to fit in with laboratory procedures—researchers recognize not signs of the spirit blowing where it listeth but rather behavior similar to other types of as yet ungovernable physical phenomena, like the movements of elementary particles.

By using recently available technology, today's physics-oriented psychic researcher hopes to come to grips with new levels of complexity in a way that his fellow of twenty or even ten years ago could not. Computers, supersensitive voltmeters, quantum counters, Faraday cages, electroencephalographs, plethysmographs and electromyographs are only a few of the new gadgets that now aid him in his quest for understanding. His microscope is focused as much upon the producer of psychic phenomena as upon the phenomena themselves, for in the end they may turn out to be one and the same. We may be witnessing not only the emergence of a new science but a new picture of physical reality to accompany it.

Back in 1905 Albert Einstein revolutionized physics with his theory of relativity, which explained previously unanswered anomalies of light and gravitation and also opened the door to the practical uses of atomic energy. Like Einstein, today's psychic researcher knows he has under his scrutiny certain facts, phenomena, processes whose existence fails to fit in with the current textbook picture of the world. They may demand an entirely new conception of time and matter, as revolutionary as Einstein's was in his day, possibly one that recognizes the mind as an intrinsic, central phenomenon in nature rather than a mere bubble floating on the surface of reality.

There have been many theories, many attempts at explaining psychic phenomena down the ages. During the seventeenth century it became fashionable to account for them by hypothetical laws of Universal Sympathy, a built-in resonance between man and the universe. In the nineteenth and early twentieth centuries psychic researchers explained them in terms of emanations and rays, or alternatively by hypothetical rods and cantilevers of ectoplasm on top of which the levitated medium wobbled. Today's psychic researcher as often as not talks in the jargon of statistics or quantum mechanics; math terms boiled dry of any meat for the imagination to flourish on, a language as obscure to most of us as classical Greek.

But this does not mean parapsychology must be a closed book to the layman. Because of its status as a pioneering science, there is still plenty of room for amateur interest. Much of what we know of psychic phenomena today is the direct result of the efforts of dedicated psychic researchers working, unfortunately, solely on an avocational basis. Even though the mathematical language used by today's psychic researcher may be beyond the grasp of the layman, it does not mean that the phenomena themselves are. Theories will always be secondary. It is facts that count, whether they be demonstrated in the laboratory or the home.

There is ample evidence that psychic ability not only lies in each and every one of us but may well constitute the very foundation of our everyday lives, although we are not aware of it. To paraphrase William James, the practical problem becomes not so much one of "how to do it," but rather of how to *get at* that elusive ability and turn it from a suspicion into a reality.

My aim in this book is to provide the reader with a working

guide for exploring some of these avenues of research for himself, albeit with the proviso that he be content to leave experimental fine points to the professional parapsychologist.

I have tried throughout to put everything in simple terms, avoiding where possible technical jargon, which frequently conceals more than it reveals. Obviously, to fasten a scientific-sounding name to something does not necessarily explain it. Useful terms like ESP, however, which are embedded in the parapsychologist's vocabulary, do appear and are fully explained, both in the text and in the glossary.

No specialized equipment is needed for the majority of the experiments described here, other than what can easily be improvised. The chief apparatus required for psychic research the reader possesses already—the most complex device known to man:

his own mind.

TWO

Understanding ESP

Exactly what is ESP, why do we have it and what can we do with it? Can parapsychologists tell us anything definite and useful about it?

The answer is yes—up to a point.

Down the years experimental observations have been made about our psychic powers. Though many of them show consistent patterns, the inferences drawn from them remain for the most part speculative. Their psychological and physical correlates have only comparatively recently begun to be measured with any accuracy. Therefore any statements about ESP describe for the most part only how it appears to us on the surface. Its real nature may turn out to be quite different from what we expected when a parapsychological Einstein finally comes along and fits all the pieces of the jigsaw together. What we experience as telepathy or clairvoyance may well be the tip of an iceberg whose bulk we may never, even in our wildest imaginings, have envisaged. Has parapsychological theorizing been too timid so far, too conservatively based on the commonsense point of view? Only time and further research will tell. But with some of the information parapsychologists have come up with over the years, we can at least form a general rationale for ourselves, even though it may not be a strictly scientific one. Let us therefore start with a few definitions.

WHAT IS PSYCHIC RESEARCH?

Psychic is a word deriving from the Greek *psyche*, meaning "soul." It was coined at the end of the nineteenth century as a term to cover instances of alleged thought transference, true dreams, communication from the dead, astral projection, poltergeists, levitation and (in those days) hypnotism. Its systematic investigation was the pursuit of three now-famous privately sponsored organizations of scholars and scientists: the English and American Societies for Psychical Research, and in France the Institut Métapsychique Internationale. It was accorded permanent academic status during the 1930's with the establishment of the Parapsychology Laboratory at Duke University, Durham, North Carolina, under the direction of Dr. Joseph Banks Rhine, then associate professor of psychology. Dr. Rhine started his investigation of psychic phenomena with tests to establish statistically the reality of mind-to-mind thought transference, employing a technique unsuccessfully tried at Stanford University at the beginning of the century, along lines suggested by Dr. Charles Richet of the Institut Métapsychique.

The technique, as I described earlier, involved having one person, the "sender," look at a series of twenty-five cards while another, the "receiver," wrote down his guesses of what they were. But unlike the Stanford University experiments, those at Duke turned up a high percentage of correct guesses, which led Dr. Rhine to speculate that they were being obtained by some type of sixth sense of the receiver. He named this inferred faculty *extrasensory perception*, ESP for short. Today, however, many parapsychologists prefer to use the word *psi* instead.

WHY PSI?

Psi—pronounced "sigh"—is the Greek letter ψ, which forms the prefix of words like *psychic* and *psychology*. It was coined back in 1942 as a handy umbrella term to cover the entire range of all our psychic powers by two English psychic researchers, Robert H. Thouless, onetime president of the (English) Society for Psychical Research, and biochemist B. P. Wiesner. They offered it as a less specific alternative to Rhine's ESP. They were less sure than Rhine that what was being measured in his card-guessing tests was, in fact, perception. It was extrasensory all right, but could you in all honesty call a guess perception? Perception implies a subject-object relationship plus conscious awareness, which is exactly what Rhine's ESP tests did *not* seem to demonstrate. His subjects became aware that ESP had occurred only at the end of the test. The ESP process was an entirely unconscious one and remained so unless something like a coincidence of cards and guesses happened, allowing one to infer some kind of mental transmission.

Today's parapsychologists, while still retaining the term *ESP* for convenience, have adopted the more cautious word. R. A. McConnell, research professor of biophysics at the University of Pittsburgh and a leading light in the field of parapsychology, defines ESP as "a response to an unknown event not presented to any known sense." [1] When stated like that, it admittedly begins to sound a little like one of those black cats blind philosophers are accused of searching dark rooms for. But then, a well-turned scientific axiom is not noted for its fancy imagery but rather for its lack of it.

Paranormal cognition is another term you run across in parapsychology today. *Cognition* simply means "knowing," and *paranormal* implies "natural" but not "normal." It's a useful term, but as a definition of ESP it may turn out to be a little misleading. First, it's not always "knowing," and, second, many parapsychologists are coming around to the opinion that psi is both a natural and normal faculty, albeit a remarkably reticent one.

THE CHARACTERISTICS OF PSI

Psi may be universal. Recent experiments performed in Europe and the United States indicate that other animals besides man possess psi. Cats, rodents, and chickens give evidence of it.[2] This observation leads one to speculate whether psi may be a primary type of perception, part of our basic equipment for dealing with our environment. Perhaps it is the same mechanism that colonies of insects use, in combination with chemical signals, to coordinate their activities; a phenomenon that has long baffled scientists. Parapsychologists wonder whether psi may not perform a dual function: first as a type of blueprint of shared *experience* for a species to accompany the biological DNA code, and second as a primitive sensing and manipulative mechanism.[3] A mechanism of this sort would naturally fall into disuse as the organism evolved into a more complex form and produced external organs, like hands, eyes and ears, better suited than psi power for dealing with things in its immediate environment. Psi would vanish from conscious use when the creatures learned how to communicate with one another in speech and strengthened their hold over the external world by improvising tools for themselves. It is a matter of observation that members of primitive societies who employ unsophisticated, nonanalytical languages often seem to be more in touch with their ESP powers than we are.[4] That is not to say our ESP withers away altogether once we attain an analytical level of reasoning. Recent experiments have strongly indicated that we almost certainly use it all the time without being aware of the fact.[5]

PSI AS A FIELD PHENOMENON

Ultimate privacy. It's a nice ideal, but when examined under the microscope of science, it turns out to be rather illusory. For, as the poet John Donne sagely observed over three hundred years ago, "No man is an Island entire of itself." We may look as though we are isolated from one another by a layer of skin, a wedge of air and then another layer of skin, but our isolation is more apparent than real. Scientists have known for a long time that what we think of as a largely empty world filled with apparently isolated objects like you and me is really a network of pulsating, flashing radiations in all shades of the energy spectrum.

Ignorance, however, is quite obviously bliss. We are only aware of the narrow section that appears to us as light. X rays, gamma rays, cosmic rays and radio waves zip by and through us, generally without our being any the wiser, unless as occasionally can happen we start picking up local radio stations with the metal fillings in our teeth! Not only are we immersed in a flood of for the most part invisible radiation, but we also generate our own to add to the confusion. Every nervous impulse in our bodies, every message sent by the eye to the brain or the brain to the hand is really a long chain of electrical pulses, bursts of electrons playing tag along the corridors of our nerves. Every atom in our bodies, moreover, clings to its neighbor by means of electronic interaction. Our entire physical frames, from the point of view of an electron, are nothing more than vast, buzzing webs of electrical energy.

Electromagnetic fields generated by all this electrical activity extend, cocoonlike, to a distance of several feet beyond our bodies, something long suspected but only recently given corroborative backing in the laboratory.[6] As we are able to use electromagnetic waves to transport radio messages from one end of the world to the other, may not our ESP turn out to be a form of biological radio, dependent upon our own bodies' electromagnetic fields? Mental radio, in effect?

If only it were, how much easier ESP would be to understand! Psi, alas, appears to be essentially a nonelectrical phenomenon, despite the many attempts over the years by parapsychologists to prove it so. Isolating psychics in Faraday cages (electrified rooms lined with copper that shield anything inside from any type of electromagnetism) has not lessened their ESP abilities. They continue to pick up psi impressions from the outside world just as merrily as ever.[7]

However, this does not exclude the possibility of *other* types of energy fields from being the ESP message carriers. Back in 1964 William G. Roll, the present project director of the Psychical Research Foundation, a privately financed parapsychological organization in Durham, North Carolina, suggested that an energy field of some sort would best explain the experimental measurements he had been making of science-defying instances of poltergeist pranks.

We shall be taking a closer look at his theory in later chapters. Suffice it to say for now that such a psi-field theory provides a handy rationale not only for poltergeist activity but also for ESP.[8] What the "psi energy" in the field could be is anybody's guess. So far it has not been detected by mechanical means. But then, if it really is nonelectromagnetic, regular electronic apparatus would stand about as much chance of trapping it as a sieve does water!

PSI AS A DUAL PROCESS

Psi energy then, if we can call it that for the time being, seems to have two distinct ways in which it shows itself in us: It can travel toward us or away from us. Or, put in another way and using radio as an analogy, two types of psi signal can occur: an incoming signal, which we call ESP, where we function as a sort of psychic radio receiver; or an outgoing signal known as PK, short for psychokinesis. This is another Rhine word, referring to the demonstrated power our minds have to move or interfere with distant objects; our ability to function as a psychic broadcasting unit, if you like. Both ESP and PK are classified as psi phenomena, although powerful PK effects like psychic healing and Roll's poltergeist activity appear to involve other physical energies as well.

THREE TYPES OF ESP

Splitting ESP into types is an old game indulged in by parapsychologists, and unfortunately it often tends to lead around and around the mulberry bush, as we shall see.

There are principally two sources from which our ESP

appears to gather its information: people and things. These give us our first two types of ESP: telepathy and clairvoyance.

TELEPATHY

When we pick up psi impressions from the minds of other people—their thoughts—parapsychologists say we are exercising our psi power in the form of *telepathy*. This is a term invented in 1882 by Frederic Myers, one of the founders of the first scientifically oriented psychic research organization, the original Society for Psychical Research in England.

When for no apparent reason you know what someone is going to say before he says it, or you pick up the phone to call your wife and she's already on the line calling you, you may well be exercising telepathy. At any rate, when it does happen spontaneously, this is often the form it takes.

People generally find telepathy the easiest of the psi manifestations to accept. After all, some sort of biological radio, electromagnetic or not, does make a certain amount of sense. You can even fit it into your old physics textbook picture of the world without too much of a stretch of the imagination.

CLAIRVOYANCE

The second source of our psi impressions is things rather than minds. *Clairvoyance*, a French word meaning "clear-seeing," paradoxically often has nothing to do with any type of visual imagery.

Researchers began to consider clairvoyance seriously as a measurable phenomenon back in the 1930's when Dr. Rhine discovered that higher-than-chance scores could be obtained by card guessers even when the experimenters did *not* look at the cards but simply dealt them face downward in sequence.[9] Psychics and mediums had been claiming the power of X-ray vision for years, but here at last was supportive statistical evidence of a direct mind-to-matter link, as opposed to mind-to-mind telepathy.

Clairvoyance is more difficult for the newcomer to parapsychology to accept than telepathy. Telepathy, in a way, stands to reason. Obviously the human brain is a mysterious black box humming with undisclosed secrets, one of which could well be the power to communicate extrasensorily with other brains. But how on earth can a brain pick up information *directly* from, say, the interior of a locked box, which is in fact what happens in clairvoyance? Sadly, we have to dump our convenient mental-radio analogy for psi at this point.

All is not lost, however. Radar, another closely related type of communication system, offers us an equally good analogy, and it's also applicable to telepathy, which some para-psychologists today feel is just another type of clairvoyance exercised between the mind of the percipient and the physical brain of the sender.

A radar set combines the function of radio transmitter and receiver in one instrument. Radio signals are emitted, bounced off the distant object inquired about, and their echoes caught and traced on a screen for all to see. Maybe clairvoyance is a type of biological radar? What part of the target does our unseen psi beam strike, then? A number of recent experiments indicate that what is most often picked up by this psi beam appears to be the cluster of psi impressions derived from other people previously associated with the target rather than anything special about the object itself.[10] Strictly speaking, then, this is a type of telepathy by proxy, and it is usually referred to by psychic researchers as *psychometry*, or object reading. (I warned you this was a mulberry bush!)

It would be very convenient to say that this explains the hard part about clairvoyance, namely that annoying mind-to-matter link. Unfortunately it does not. Certain square pegs still remain, which at first sight obstinately refuse to fit this neat round hole. A phenomenon known as dowsing, or water witching, is one of them. This long-attested ability of some people to divine the whereabouts of underground water or metal by means of the movement of a rod or pendulum held in the hand cannot be explained away by this proxy telepathy theory. Unless someone once knew of the whereabouts of the hidden water, where would the ESP impression come from?

Apparently psi must react directly to geological configurations too, or at least to radiations given off by matter, in this case the underground water. This is the theory that dowsers themselves favor most. However, we shouldn't jump to conclusions hastily.

There remains one more possible explanation, and it takes us off in a new direction, introducing us to what is probably one of the most eerie and disturbing of all psi phenomena. Obviously no one has previously seen the dowser's target. But someone *might*, in the future; namely, the dowser himself. Is it possible that, in some way, he might be reacting to psi impressions coming from his *future* knowledge? One's mind boggles at the idea at first. Effects preceding causes? It sounds a little like hauling oneself aloft by one's shoelaces. Interestingly enough, however, it is only you and I who have fixed ideas about the rigidly one-way-only nature of time. Physicists have been quietly standing time on its head for years. In fact, some of their most abstruse equations can be translated as the notion that electrons can actually travel *backward* in time.[11] Albert Einstein did a lot to prepare the ground for the general loosening of scientists' attitudes toward time with his Special Theory of Relativity back in 1905. Not only did he state (and later prove) that the time duration of an object—how long it exists—was as real an attribute as its length, depth and width, but, more astonishingly, that each and every one of these measurements, physical and chronological, could shift in magnitude depending on where one happened to be measuring from—expanding and contracting in accordance with the object's velocity in the universe relative to one's own.

If, then, time is as physical a thing as length and width, and if we can observe things happening up and down the road outside our house, maybe we can somehow become aware of what is going on up the time road too, if not with our five senses, then with our ESP. It so happens that we can, and the name given by parapsychologists to this sort of psi spying into the future is *precognition*, which simply means "foreknowledge."

PRECOGNITION

Statistically significant signs of precognition put in an appearance in Dr. Rhine's laboratory tests soon after those of clairvoyance, back in the early 1930's. Rhine discovered that his card guessers were correctly guessing cards *before* they had been selected.[12] He realized immediately that all his preconceived ideas about telepathy and clairvoyance might now have to be thrown out the window. For instance, what had until now been considered clairvoyance might turn out to be *precognitive* telepathy: picking up psi impressions coming *back* in time from one's own, or the experimenter's, future knowledge after the results of the test had been checked! One's common sense bucks a bit at this proposition, but given the potential of precognition, it did present a distinct possibility.

For a while it looked as though any attempt to make hard and fast boundaries between telepathy, clairvoyance and precognition was doomed to failure. However, in 1936 a radio engineer named G. N. M. Tyrrell cleverly managed to construct an experiment that isolated clairvoyance and demonstrated its claim as an independent ESP phenomenon. Tyrrell hit upon the ingenious idea of using a machine to match the guesses against randomly selected targets automatically and, while retaining the totals of correct and incorrect responses, discard the original targets so that no future psi impressions of them could ever feed back into the past as precognitive telepathy. Clairvoyance was then indeed seen to be a fact.[13]

Of course precognition has been knocking around for several thousand years under the aliases of prophecy and soothsaying. Only recently have parapsychologists begun to consider it seriously as a "tamable" type of ESP, chiefly because of the difficulty of fitting it into an experimental format. Some of the most spectacular precognition experiments to date were performed in 1969 by Stanley Krippner, Montague Ullman and Charles Honorton with the assistance of an English psychic named Malcolm Bessent, who had a history of correct precognitive experiences. Under controlled laboratory conditions, Bessent recounted his dreams on eight consecutive nights. A number of dream topics were then randomly selected by another experimenter who was kept in ignorance of Bessent's recorded dreams. These randomly selected topics were then acted out by the experimenter, who made use of suitable art prints and props to supply the relevant imagery, even playing recorded background music in appropriate instances.

When descriptions of the dreams were compared with descriptions of the randomly contrived "happenings," five direct hits out of eight trials were seen to have been obtained. Five of Bessent's dreams corresponded exactly with five of the "special waking experiences" selected *after* he had finished the dream series.[14]

How can one rationalize precognition? Clairvoyance was hard enough. One of the most helpful pictorial props we can use is our time-road analogy. You want to see what is happening several miles ahead of you up the winding road, but the hedges and curves prevent this. Your best plan is to climb a nearby telephone pole or tree. Geometrically, you will be moving your visual vantage point up out of the plane and gaining perspective. Likewise with precognition. If you think of yourself as a being existing in four dimensions—namely, width, depth, height and time duration—then the only way you are going to see what is happening to you, say, a year hence is by moving your mental vantage point out into some unimaginable fifth dimension, in this way creating a view of your time road into the future. Precognition shows us that the psi part of us is able, somehow, to move out into this hypothetical fifth dimension in the same way that our three-dimensional bodies are able to climb the telephone pole.

What *really* happens during precognition? It's all very well to come up with pat ideas like "looking up the time road," but obviously such an explanation won't do for a scientist. Trying to fit precognition into a scientific framework automatically launches one into a dizzying world of quantum mechanics, hypothetical particles and relativity physics. Various attempts have been made at building mathematical models to explain it, but none of them is exactly what one might call illuminating to the layman.[15]

Interestingly enough, it is this very problem—what on earth to do about precognition—that divides psychic research into its two chief contrasting schools of thought today. On the one hand stand those led by Rhine, who favor what can be called a metaphysical explanation—they feel that physics can never hope to come to terms with the phenomena. On the other hand stand those less radical, like the philosopher C. W. K. Mundle, who feel the explanation of psi may lie within a physics not necessarily confined by its present theoretical boundaries.[16] Their differences in the end may turn out to be semantic, more apparent than real, a matter of from whose point of view the psi phenomena are observed: man's-eye view (parapsychology) or atom's-eye view (paraphysics). Today's physics has not come up with an explanation for precognition, but that is no guarantee that tomorrow's won't.

For the time being, then, most of us must content ourselves with the knowledge that precognition happens, as men once had to accept the inexplicable reality of hairs being drawn to amber before the principle of static electricity was defined. Perhaps we can comfort ourselves with the realization that understanding the physics of precognition probably won't help us peer into the future to forestall unwelcome events, any more than understanding the electromagnetic nature of light can teach near-sighted people to see better.

So these, then, are the three principal shapes our ESP comes in. Telepathy, clairvoyance, and precognition. A fourth is sometimes included, so-called *retrocognition*—psi spying the distant past—but this usually can be explained as psychometry, the awareness of past events being derived from psi impressions associated with an object or place (about which we shall have more to say later).

THE PHYSICAL LIMITS OF ESP

But are the much-touted powers of ESP really unlimited? Scientists hold dear a principle known as the Law of Conservation of Energy, and one of the chief causes of antipathy toward even the *idea* of ESP is the threat it seems to pose to that principle. In practical terms the law boils down to: "You can't get something for nothing." Action and counteraction always balance out; work done must be paid for in energy. ESP, however, is not a perpetual motion machine. It, too, obeys physical laws, although we are not too sure how those laws are to be formulated.

For instance, many experiments have been performed over the years with the intention of nailing down just what effect, if any, physical distance has on the strength of an ESP signal. Rhine himself performed several. One of the most intriguing to date was undertaken in 1965 by mathematicians Karlis Osis and M. E. Turner, Jr., using newly developed techniques of information theory to evaluate their results. Osis and Turner found that the accuracy of their subjects' guesses did in fact diminish with increased distance between them and the targets, as some of the earlier experiments had also indicated. But whereas previous experimenters failed to come up with a consistent formula that would predict the rate of ESP signal fading, Osis and Turner came up with one that they called the Inverse Two-fifths Law.

ESP signals, like light and radio waves, seem to decrease in intensity over a distance. However, unlike light and radio waves, whose intensity declines in inverse proportion to the distance between transmitter and receiver multiplied by itself, Osis and Turner observed that the ESP signal seemed to fade out at a less steep rate, roughly inversely proportional to *two-fifths* of the distance between transmitter and receiver—in this case between psychic and target. In other words, the scores declined by a little less than the inverse square root of the distance.

Osis and Turner performed their tests with subjects whose distance from the target material ranged from a hundred yards to thousands of miles—New York to Tasmania was the farthest stretch. They assumed that the ESP signals would travel around the circumference of the earth as radio waves do. However, knowing what we do about the ability of ESP signals to slip through electromagnetic traps like Faraday cages, there is no real reason why they should not take the shorter route, and instead of plodding along around the planetary curve, zoom right through the ground under our feet. If photons—infinitesimally small elementary particles that bunch together to form light and radio waves—do not perform the task of carrying our ESP messages as they do our radio-borne voices, there are plenty of other elementary particles around that might do the job just as well, if not better.

Take the neutrino, for instance. The neutrino is about as antisocial a particle as you can get. In the parlance of physicists, it has no measurable rest mass to grab onto and no attractive electric charge, which gives it carte blanche to go just about anywhere in the universe it pleases. If waves of neutrinos whizzing through space turned out to be carriers of ESP messages, as several parapsychologists have suggested, then not only would the thickest of lead barriers fail to deflect them but the entire earth would provide as much of an obstacle to them as butter does to a hot knife. Obviously, if psi signals can pass through the ground, the ESP distance-decline ratio may turn out to be different from the one proposed by Osis and Turner.[17] But my point in mentioning these experiments here is that, whatever the ratio ultimately turns out to be, they demonstrate fairly clearly that ESP *does* obey physical laws of some sort. They put to rest once and for all the old criticism that quantitative evidence of ESP represents merely some odd quirk in the laws of statistics themselves.[18]

If, as it now appears, ESP is subject to some form of physical attenuation, then the same may well be true of precognition—the span of time our psi can probe into the future. Inasmuch as psi is a natural phenomenon, boundaries and limitations of some sort obviously do exist. But, as our astrophysicists now know, the faintest type of signal—in their case a radio signal coming from the farthermost corner of the galaxy—can be pinpointed, amplified and made intelligible, provided you know just where to look for it. The same may be true for ESP. Many examples of the exercise of ESP over enormous intercontinental distances exist in the records of parapsychology. There is even possible evidence of an interplanetary one on record! [19] The task of psi focusing—our ability to zero in on targets—is obviously an extremely important factor in the ESP process. What we lack in ESP voltage we may well make up for in our tuning capacity. The vistas opened by this possibility could be, one day, quite literally astronomical in their scope.

ESP IN OUR DAILY LIVES

This is all fine, you may say, but what has psi got to do with me? Apart from an occasional flash of what *might* have been telepathy, I've never experienced it. Warning dreams and odd psychic occurrences only happen to other people.

That is what you may think, but you are probably quite wrong. What appears on the surface, the so-called commonsense point of view, is not always the truth of the matter. We all have remarkably little knowledge about what is really going on deep down inside us most of the time. We may think we act in a rational and carefully thought out manner, but very rarely do we allow ourselves to become aware of all the subconscious lobbying that goes on all the time within us to tip the balance in favor of one course of action over another. If we *were* sometimes acting on ESP-derived information, how many of us would be aware of the fact? Very few. Only those individuals whom we call ESP sensitives or psychics would: people who have found themselves able, by some mysterious means, to dredge up their psi reactions and objectify them as a hunch or a vision.

One of the things parapsychologists have begun to suspect from repeated observation is that ESP, far from being a rare occurrence, is something that is not only latent in all of us but is going on all the time, even though we happen to be blissfully unaware of the fact. It would be equally true to say that ESP is not something we *do* but rather something that continually *happens* to us. When we *do* it we are really just turning our attention to something that is already there. According to our field-theory rationale, our individual psi fields are constantly meshing and interacting together, picking up this and that from each other. Maybe this is the explanation of that well-known phenomenon of ideas "floating" or being "in the air."

Authors are painfully aware of this situation. You sit down to express yourself on paper one day, only to pick up a new book or magazine article the following day and read the same ideas and sometimes even verbatim phrases. According to our theory, one's psi field has obligingly and quite amorally sought out and lifted the relevant information from the other author's psi field, a possible reinforcing factor being a precognitive link with the printed book or article.

Psychotherapists at times become very aware of this type of mental osmosis happening between themselves and their patients. The unspoken preoccupations of one will unexpectedly and sometimes embarrassingly show up in the dreams of the other.[20] ESP-induced dreams of this type seem to provide a bridge between patient and therapist, or a pretext for discussion, which often amounts to the same thing. Accordingly, they seem to crop up when the patient begins to fear the loss of contact with his helper.

It seems likely that our psychic feelers responsible for this type of mental seepage do not spend their time waving vaguely in all directions just for the sheer fun of it. Like all of our life processes they may well have evolved in response to some sort of need. Unlike science-fiction writers, who generally seem to view psi as a newly emerging faculty in man, many parapsychologists today feel that it represents not necessarily a vestigial remnant like body hair but a primitive information-gathering and action-performing ability later superseded by the evolution of immediately practical sense organs and limbs for locomotion and manipulation. But the faculty still remains there, deep down inside every one of us, unobtrusively performing its own special tasks clairvoyantly or telepathically, retro- or precognitively as the need may be, acting as a biological scanning mechanism and sniffing out things that, again deep down, we may need although perhaps unconsciously. Like animals perpetually in search of food, our psi fields constantly sniff out what parapsychologist Rex Stanford has called our "need-relevant circumstances"—things, events, information, even people, that in some deep way fit our life pattern and support us, often by reflecting or justifying our psychological states to ourselves.[5]

Probably all of us at some time in our lives have been aware of periods when lucky breaks occurred; when we really seemed to be in tune with fate; when lucky coincidence followed lucky coincidence. Things that unaccountably happen in twos and threes, a frequently observed phenomenon, become a little more understandable in the light of this theory, too. Our ESP scanning process, if we can call it that, picks out a theme, name, person, and harps on it or them in response to some deeply felt need. Consciously you may not be aware of what this need is—why, for instance, a certain name you haven't heard in years keeps popping up out of the blue—but your inner "you" does, and it may be worth your while to try to identify your need by asking yourself a few soul-searching questions.

Primitive societies, perhaps with more astuteness than we credit them for, generally look on extraordinary coincidences as omens: signs from spirits or gods pointing toward a certain course of action. Frequently such signs are received in the form of symbolic dreams, often of a warning nature, indicating a death or some equally important matter.

The psychologist C. G. Jung was very aware of this type of phenomenal coincidence. He thought it defied physical explanation and coined a new word for it, *synchronicity*, by which he meant an occurrence of acausal coincidence; that is, one in which no connection existed between the two events other than their equivalence of *meaning*, which he took to be a universal principle as active as physical causality: a type of "birds-of-a-feather-flock-together" cosmic force. Jung wrote a book about synchronicity in conjunction with none other than the discoverer of the neutrino, Wolfgang Pauli. In it he described a classic example of this type of coincidence:

> I noted the following on April 1, 1949: Today is Friday. We have fish for lunch. Somebody happens to mention the custom of making an "April fish" of someone. That same morning I made a note of an inscription which read: "Est homo totus medius *piscis* ab imo." In the afternoon a former patient of mine, whom I had not seen in months, showed me some extremely impressive pictures of fish which she had painted in the meantime. In the evening I was shown a piece of embroidery with fish-like sea-monsters in it. On the morning of April 2 another patient, whom I had not seen for many years, told me a dream in which she stood on the shore of a lake and saw a large fish that swam straight towards her and landed at her feet. I was at the time engaged on a study of the fish symbol in history. Only one of the persons mentioned here knew anything about it.[21]

Maybe Jung's intense study of the fish symbol, which at the time was full of significance for him, served to put his psychic scanning process on the alert. It not only led him to literary references about the subject, but because of the emotional bond forged previously between him and his former patients, it allowed their psi fields to pick it up and register it in the form of dreams, embroidery subjects and paintings. Or to put it another way, the symbol was in the air, although Jung never recognized the phenomenon as his own doing.

"LUCK"—THE CONSTRUCTIVE OR DESTRUCTIVE USE OF OUR ESP

Self-help books nearly always make Positive Thinking the sine qua non for the bigger, better, healthier, wealthier, lovelier, happier, more effective or whatever other improved type of life they advocate. Strange as it may seem to the person who feels no need for that type of book, they are right. Positive thinking often does appear to work. Psychologists, however, have a rather different explanation from the cosmic or divine influence usually cited as responsible for the beneficial results. They ascribe them to the power of *autosuggestion*, an amazing capacity we all possess of being able to alter the way our own brains think, act and even perceive things. As we shall see in later chapters, it is this same ability, so simple in itself but so powerful in effect, that is used by psychics to uncover and encourage their psychic faculties.

The chief use of the autosuggestion proposed by self-help books is to induce in us a positive mental attitude toward our lives and fellows. Even psychologists of the most no-nonsense category agree that a positive attitude is a healthy one. Psychotherapists spend most of their time trying to help their patients to achieve just such a state of, if not manic optimism, at least of positive and aware yea-saying to life.

What they frequently do not take into account, however, is the psi factor involved in their patients' constitutions. While not necessarily endorsing the "think-yourself-to-fame-and-riches" line of the self-help books, a number of parapsychologists are today coming to the conclusion that our mental attitudes not only make us more prone to invent good or bad situations for ourselves, but actually lead us toward them—or stranger still, attract them to us.

It's a rather disturbing idea when you come to think about it. Jesus was alleged to have said that those who had would get more, and those who didn't have would lose even what they had; a rather baffling statement on the face of it, which has been interpreted as everything from an indictment of capitalism to a counsel of spiritual poverty. It could equally well be read as a recognition that our deepest-held opinion of ourselves does in fact affect our "luck," bringing to us in our daily lives what we feel we need or deserve. If we have been conditioned to think of ourselves as losers, losers we often remain. Even if a lucky break does occur, we'll find a way of lousing it up. Conversely, winners go on winning.

Charisma of this sort, alas, seems to have nothing to do with morals or ethics. It may simply be a matter of psychological orientation: how we have learned or been conditioned to think of ourselves. The reasons *why* we attract good or bad luck to ourselves are hidden and obviously extremely complex, differing in the case of each individual. They can best be rooted out by the psychoanalyst, whose special province they are. However, speaking very broadly, the problem often appears to hinge on a question of self-justification. Maybe if we believe we need to justify our pessimistic view of the world, our psi will lead us into situations that do just that: possibly not in the obvious sense of falling off ladders or missing trains (although that may be part of the pattern), but rather by continually leading us into situations where the bad luck appears to come from an external agency. Deals always falling through at the last moment; calamity hovering at every turn of the way; always being in the wrong place at the wrong time; a repeated pattern of frustration or failure—these are more likely to be indicators of psi at work. Even if we may not ourselves be cursed with this bad-luck syndrome, we all know people who are.

Psychologists often find such people to be more than normally laden with guilts and inhibitions imposed upon them early on in life, with a consequent low opinion of themselves and, springing from this, self-destructive tendencies. In this instance the pattern of disaster often appears to act as an attention-getting device directed at their friends and relatives.

Equally unfortunate are the psychic "losers" who are stuck with what is known to psychologists as an approach-avoidance conflict. They repeatedly find they can go only so far in a project or a personal relationship. Then, because of an often un-conscious fear of disillusionment or inadequacy, a seemingly inevitable reverse tendency begins to make itself felt, and they begin to find circumstances mysteriously conspiring to prevent its completion or consolidation.

If our own unconscious psi *is* leading us into, or organizing, these sorts of situations, as parapsychologist Rex Stanford has suggested, maybe in some convoluted way we are deriving some type of benefit from it, be it justification of an ingrained negative belief about oneself or a demonstration of how needful one is for someone else's attention, which often amounts to the same thing.[22]

A psychic luck theory like this is obviously open to all sorts of misinterpretations. Psi karma of this sort cannot be used as a catchall excuse to account for all the misery in the world. Someone born with multiple sclerosis obviously is cursed by a malfunction of nature, not his own psi power. But for those of us who, *for no apparent reasons*, seem to be born winners or losers, there remains the possibility that our luck is in some measure attributable to the hidden workings of our own psi fields.

At least from a psychic point of view, then, there is every reason in the world why each of us should take the self-help books' advice seriously and set about getting it all together in order to focus our psi antennae in the right direction. Most of us instinctively know how to do this, I believe. We have only to observe how young children enjoy life to see the natural development of such an attitude before it becomes stunted by fears or guilts. But most of us also need to relearn from our own kids. Learning to stop resisting, to adopt an attitude of optimistic openness toward daily life, is a good place to start. Cultivating a realization of one's own intrinsic worth as a human being, however bad or foolish one has been made to feel by others in the past, is another good guideline. Learning the knack of applying yourself to achieving what *you yourself* consider worthwhile goals is a third.

If these propositions sound naive and nonoccult, they are nonetheless valid rules for daily life. In the same way that psi seems to be an absolutely integral part of our lives, a well-developed capacity to make use of psi may spring from a well-developed capacity for living.

THREE

Demonstrating ESP for Yourself

For most of us psi remains a buried power, albeit under our noses—a type of primitive ESP scanning process. But you don't have to take my word for its existence. One of the best ways of demonstrating this ESP activity to yourself and your friends is with a picture-drawing test. They are extremely easy to do and can be highly entertaining. No mathematics are required, because these are what parapsychologists call *qualitative* tests; that is, one-of-a-kind tests that are concerned with the *quality* of the ESP or PK being produced rather than the *quantity*.

The test I am going to describe here is a variation on the one mentioned in Chapter One. Picture-drawing tests are nearly always successful to some degree or other, which accounts for their popularity among psychic researchers even after their place in the laboratory limelight was taken by the quantitative card-guessing tests of Dr. Rhine. Attempts have been made to fit them into a quantitative framework by scoring each drawing for degrees of success, but the number of variables and qualifications one ends up with can be large, mathematically unwieldy and rather open to debate. However, Whately Carington, a pioneering English psychic researcher of the 1940's, did set himself the task of doing such a scored series. Although the time consumed by his experiment was enormous, the positive results he achieved showed evidence of psi like that found in card-guessing tests.[1]

Many famous parapsychologists and psychic researchers past and present have experimented with simple picture-drawing tests. There are several books on the subject that are considered classics of parapsychology.[2] One of the most famous, *Mental Radio*, was written by Upton Sinclair in 1930. It details three years of successful picture-drawing experiments he carried out with his wife. So intrigued was Albert Einstein by what Sinclair had to say that the great scientist wrote an introduction to the book, in which he underlined the significance of the phenomena described within its pages.

Interestingly enough, Einstein's insights have a knack of being about forty years ahead of the rest of the world. His 1905 equation of mass and energy was dramatically and incontrovertibly displayed at Hiroshima in 1945. The ascendance of parapsychology as a science appears to have truly begun around 1970, some forty years after Einstein's introduction to *Mental Radio*.

DEMONSTRATING ESP SCANNING

To conduct an ESP drawing test, you really don't have to be able to draw. So long as you can wield a pencil and make a shape on paper, you are qualified. However, as with many ESP experiments, you will have to find a partner to help you. Try to find someone whom you can relax with. Age, sex or relationship doesn't matter, but other factors may affect your score. Ideally, your partner should at least be open to the *idea* of ESP, even if he or she has never actually seen any evidence of it. It also helps if you can apply one or more of the following descriptive adjectives to him or her. (We shall see why later.)

warm	adventuresome
sociable	quick
good-natured	carefree
enthusiastic	emotional
talkative	practical

cheerful	self-assured
alert	relaxed
responsive	easygoing

The more of these terms that are applicable, the greater your chances of getting good results. If *both* you and your partner happen to be this type of person, your chances are better still.

To take the test, you should each have, first, a pad of paper and a pencil or ball-point pen. Then pick an opportune time when neither of you is tired or distracted. As this is not a laboratory test but only a demonstration, you can both be in the same room, albeit on opposite sides and facing opposite directions. However, if you have two rooms at your disposal, make use of them. The scribbling sounds made by the pencils on the paper can be distracting if not informative of the type of picture you are drawing.

When you are both seated comfortably, clearly mark the top sheet number 1 and begin your first sketch. Draw anything that comes into your head. If nothing comes into your head, put your pencil point on the paper and take it for a walk, improvising and embellishing on the pattern it makes as you go along. Try to keep your drawing bold and obvious.

Tell your partner to begin his drawing after you have had a minute or two at yours. He should also clearly mark his drawing number 1. Your partner will sometimes start incorporating the material scanned by ESP from you almost immediately, although sometimes it takes a drawing or two before the psi-scanned material begins filtering through. Sometimes it works the other way around: you may subsequently find you began modifying *your* drawing to correspond to his. Two to three minutes is usually enough time for each sketch—don't try for masterpieces.

When both of you decide you've done enough on a sketch, begin the next. Again, this should be numbered clearly. Five or six drawings are usually enough for your first sequence. Then reverse roles. Let your partner begin, and you start after a minute or two. Again, make five or six sketches, coordinating your efforts verbally and numbering each of them carefully before you start drawing. Do not compare them until you finish both sequences.

ANALYZING YOUR RESULTS

If everything goes according to plan, when you check your drawings you may note that those of the lead draftsman introduce an image—a box or a flower, say—which has been picked up by draftsman number 2 in his drawing, or even a drawing or two later. This indicates that the ESP "flow" is obliging you by taking place in the required direction—from the lead draftsman to draftsman number 2. However, should a similarity of drawings appear between those of the lead draftsman and the previous drawings of draftsman 2, then the reverse may be true. Draftsman 1 will simply be scanning his partner's efforts from the previous sets. Or, more eerily still, draftsman 2 may be *precognizing* the sketch his partner is going to do!

It's fascinating to lay out such a drawing sequence and analyze the various elements that have ricocheted unconsciously back and forth from one experimenter to another. Occasionally you get a dead-on hit. This is very exciting when it happens, as you may find out for yourself. I tried this test some eight years ago while I was working as a set designer for BBC television. I think my partner fitted practically every one of the psi-hitting adjectives on the list above, and the results she produced turned out to be some of the most spectacular I have ever seen. (See Figures 1 to 5.)

DIFFERENCES IN DRAWINGS AND WHAT THEY MEAN

The psi-scanning process revealed here shows close kinship with the process of dreaming. One might even call it dreaming

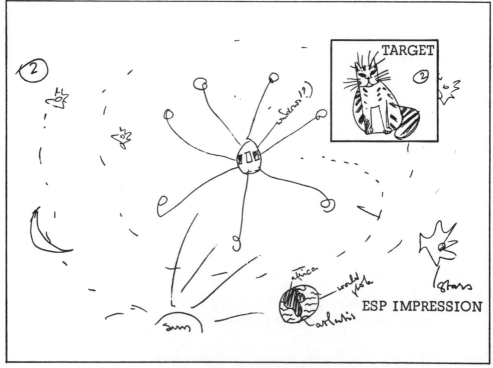

Figures 1-4. Receiver: E. Inglis-Arkell; sender: P. Huson

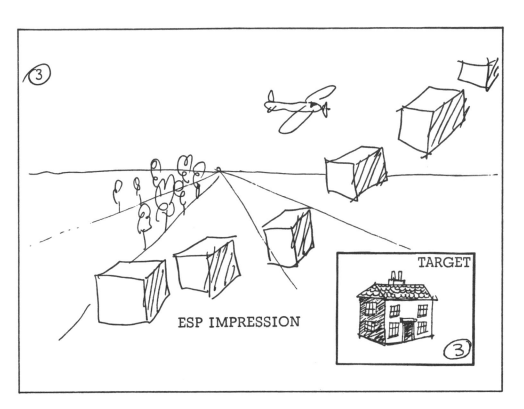

ESP IMPRESSION

TARGET

TARGET

ESP IMPRESSION

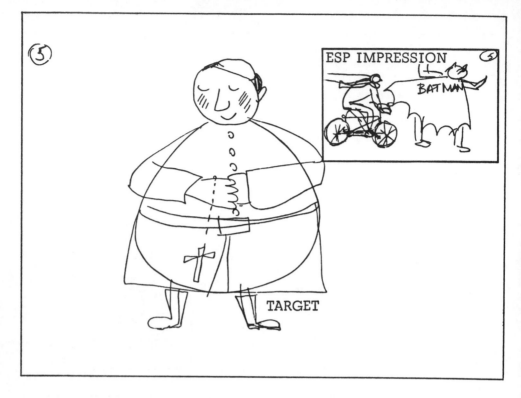

Figure 5. Receiver: P. Huson; sender: E. Inglis-Arkell

on paper. In the same way that we unconsciously weave our thoughts and emotions into tableaus and dramas every night in dreams, we seem to incorporate information scanned by our psi into the drawings.

But just as actuality usually undergoes a sea change in dreams, so our ESP messages often get twisted or transmuted. René Warcollier, a French parapsychologist who made a deep study of the dynamics involved in this process, nailed down at least seven different types of distortion that our ESP signals are subject to:

1. *Fragmentation.* A random disintegration of the signal into component parts. (See Figure 2.)

2. *Condensation.* A fusing of separate parts of the signal into a single shape.

3. *Dissociation.* An orderly dividing up of the signal into symmetrical components.

4. *Inversion.* A reversal of the target image and its ground, like a photo negative. (See Figure 4.)

5. *Multiplication.* An elaboration of the signal. (See Figure 3.)

6. *Parallelism.* A clustering together of elements similar to the signal.

7. *Synthesis.* A reconstruction of the whole signal from separate parts.[3]

These seven types of distortion crop up again and again in ESP, as you may find out for yourself. Number 6 we have encountered already in the last chapter: Jung's synchronicity. Warcollier defined one further principle, which, while not a type of distortion like the other seven, may well clue us into why the distortions happen. He named it *latency*—the observed time lag between the sending of an ESP signal and its reproduction in the receiver as a hunch, perception or involuntary action. Undoubtedly, an intricate series of hidden transactions takes place within us after we have picked up the ESP signal but before we register it, rather like the whirrings that go on in a vending machine between depositing the coin and receiving the candy bar. This ESP time lag can occur even when sender and receiver are only a few feet from one another, so distance would not appear to be a contributing factor. Rather, psi messages, even if they turn out to travel at the speed of light, need time to travel the dark corridors of the receiver's brain and nervous system before they finally emerge in recognizable form as "impressions."

Check your drawings for each one of Warcollier's distortions and note which one appears most frequently. This will probably be allied to some general psychological trait of the person who produced it.[4] From the picture-drawing tests I have tried with friends over the years, I have noted that, generally speaking, vague or emotional people tend to produce evidence of fragmentation, while analytical and deliberate types tend toward dissociation, condensation and synthesis. Exuberant and highly interested subjects often exhibit examples of multiplication and parallelism, as in Figures 1 through 4.

If you regard the sequence of drawings as a by-product of the thoughts that were passing through your mind at the time you made them, you will be able to see to what degree your thinking was open to ESP seepage. You will also note that you probably had no idea what your partner was drawing at the time. The similarities between your sketches and his are frequently restricted to *their shape alone*, with the subject matter being interpreted quite differently. For instance, you might have drawn a candle set in a candleholder, and your partner will have drawn the same shape but called it a top hat. A good example of this can be seen in Figure 2.

In this instance I drew as a target a fat, rather evil Walt Disney cat, but the percipient, while reproducing its outlines, interpreted it as a bizarre rendering of the solar system with the whiskered cat's head in the center appearing as a sputnik-type satellite. So, what you are demonstrating in these tests is obviously not *perception* in the dictionary sense of the word. It's not really *cognition*, either. It *is* a type of sharing of thoughts; a direct result of our psi scanning or the meshing together of our psi fields, however you wish to put it. It is this same ability that we must take and work up into an ESP technique for ourselves, using a few ingenious psychological tricks that we shall be discussing later.

HOW TO CONDUCT A SIMPLE CARD-GUESSING TEST

To echo Dr. Osis's words, if you are going to take parapsychology seriously, then you should know how it feels to take one of Dr. Rhine's forced-choice card-guessing tests. They can be fun to begin with, but many find this wears thin after the fourth run. There is no way around this, unfortunately, for to achieve significant results from a scientific point of view, you will have to make enough guesses for the laws of statistics to get their teeth into, so to speak.

Any type of card deck or set of symbols can be used in this

type of test. How many different symbols you have to choose from of course alters your chances of guessing correctly. Obviously, if you have a deck of cards made up of only two types of symbols, then the chances of your making a correct guess are much higher than if you were to use a deck containing as many as five different symbols. The variety of symbols used, the number of cards in the deck and the amount of runs you make with the deck are the three variable factors from which mathematicians work out the probabilities or odds for or against your end score of correct guesses.

According to the law of averages—something that has been demonstrated constantly down the ages—if you toss a coin a hundred times, it will come down tails fifty times, give or take a few. The more times you toss it, the better your chances are of predicting the outcome. Likewise, if you make several hundred attempts to pick a certain card, say a "circle," from a deck of twenty-five ESP cards containing five examples of five types of symbol, one of which is a circle, only one in five tries will on average turn out to be correct. We can express this by saying that the probability of our picking a circle by chance is one in five, 1/5, or, in decimal figures, 0.2. Parapsychologists generally consider that ESP is taking place in a test like card guessing when the mathematical probability of the correct guesses decreases to 0.01 or at the most 0.02; that is to say, one in a hundred or, at the most liberal, one in fifty instead of the chance probability of one in five. Between 0.04 and 0.02 is considered to be *suggestive* of psi though not *significant*, although most other sciences would consider a probability as high as one in twenty (0.05) sufficiently indicative of something unusual going on.

The smaller the probability number becomes, the more justified we are in the inference that the surplus of correct guesses beyond the average chance expectation is indicative of data transmission of some sort. The actual measure of success of a laboratory ESP test is given by what is known in para- psychology as a critical ratio, a sum worked out with the aid of statistical tables after the test has been completed.[5] But this type of analysis is for specialists. Provided you use the correct number of symbols and cards, you can compute your own success easily enough by adding up your hits and comparing them with the rule-of-thumb scale given below. Similarly, you don't need special ESP cards to conduct this test. Regular playing cards will do, although they only give you four types of symbol to play with as opposed to the five of the ESP deck. The type of test illustrated below is known to parapsychologists as a General ESP (GESP) Test.

PROCEDURE

Step 1

Prepare two record sheets as in Figure 6. Now, from a deck of regular playing cards select the four aces, plus twenty additional cards, five of each suit. Give one record sheet, a pencil and the four aces to the person who is going to play the part of the ESP receiver in your experiment. He should take them to another room and lay them before him on a table at which he should seat himself comfortably. While he is doing this, you, the transmitter, should shuffle the twenty selected cards and place them in a pack face down on a table in front of you.

Step 2

When you are both ready, turn over the top card and stare at it. Examine it closely, noting the roundness and redness of the symbols if they are hearts, their spiky quality if diamonds and so on. Really immerse yourself in each card and its special characteristics. While you are doing this the receiver should be letting his eyes run over the four aces before him until one of them suggests itself to him as better than the others, for whatever reason. He should not analyze *why* it does so, but simply jot down his impression in the space on the record sheet. Neither should he count the number of times he chooses the same suit during the remainder of the test.

Name: JOHN DOE   Date: 9/19/74

Type of test: GESP

Key: S=Spade, H=Heart, D=Diamond, C=Club

	RUN 1 CALL	RUN 1 CARD	RUN 2 CALL	RUN 2 CARD	RUN 3 CALL	RUN 3 CARD	RUN 4 CALL	RUN 4 CARD	RUN 5 CALL	RUN 5 CARD
1	H	D			D	H			D	S
2	H	H			H	S			D	D
3	S	H			C	D			C	H
4	D	C			D	H			S	D
5	C	C			D	D			S	S
6	S	H			H	C			H	S
7	S	D			S	C			H	S
8	C	S			S	S			C	C
9	H	H			C	C			D	C
10	H	C			C	H			H	H
11	D	D			H	H			D	H
12	C	S			H				S	D
13	H	S			S	D			S	C
14	S	D			D	D			C	S
15	S	S			H	C			D	C
16	S	C			S	S			H	C
17	D	H			C	S			C	H
18	C	S			C	C			C	H
19	C	C			S	D			S	D
20	H	D			D	S			H	S
CORE	6				-7				+11	

Figure 6. Run 1: Scored for direct hits

Run 3: Scored for one card backward displacement

Run 5: Scored for one card forward displacement

Step 3

When he has made his choice the receiver should call out to let you know. You can then turn over the next card and repeat the process.

Step 4

At the end of each run of twenty, enter the suits of the cards you have dealt into your own record sheet—bottom card first, remember.

Step 5

Reshuffle and begin your next run.

Step 6

Five runs will give you one hundred calls. When they have been completed, you can evaluate your results, entering the cards in your record sheet against the guesses in your partner's. We shall study the evaluation scale shortly.

GUESSING TECHNIQUES

When you try a test like this, the obvious question arises: How fast or slow should one guess? If latency is a factor that needs taking into account, wouldn't it be better if one were to pause between each guess long enough to allow the correct impression time to influence one's decision? How long, then, is long enough? None of these questions has a hard-and-fast answer, for obviously everyone has a different latency rate, dependent on his or her psychological makeup.

Back in 1964 American parapsychologist Rhea A. White

made an important study of the dynamics involved in the ESP process. Ms. White favored the old "wait-until-the-impression-rises" approach over the post-1930, rapid-fire "say-whatever-comes-into-your-mind" technique of Rhine's parapsychologists. Both methods, however, get results. J. G. Pratt, another colleague of Dr. Rhine, has suggested that in the "wait-until" method your psi will probably be reacting to the psi field of each of the *individual* cards, whereas in the rapid-fire method it will be responding to the overall field of the cards registered as an entire *sequence*.[6] The difference is like looking at the individual patches of color that an artist has used to make a painting, contrasted to surveying the painting as a whole. If you adopt the rapid-fire technique of, say, one card every three seconds, you may find another type of distortion turning up in your guess record when you come to check it: namely, *displacement*. This is a parapsychologist's term for guessing a card or two ahead of (or behind) the one the transmitter was concentrating on, a phenomenon attributable to latency, clairvoyance, precognition, or a combination of all three. If we consider the order of the cards as an overall pattern of symbols, rapid-fire calling might cause one's focus to slip a little out of kilter and give rise to displacement warps showing up on the record sheet. Obviously, to tell *where* the card is in sequence is as much of an ESP task as to sense the card itself.

I find my own highest scores in rapid-fire guessing of individual cards tend to come from comparing my guess with the card two places behind it; that is, guess number 3 matched with card number 1 and so on, leading me to suspect that my latency lag is around six seconds.

You may also notice that a sequence of the same card will often attract correct guesses, suggesting that the clustering of similar cards somehow reinforces their signal. It would seem to stand to reason that the ESP signal coming from one card would be affected to some degree by those coming from the cards on either side of it, strengthening it if they happened to be the same.

CHECKING YOUR RESULTS

First add up the direct hits you have scored and compare them with the evaluation scale. Then check the guesses for backward or forward displacements; that is, against one or two cards behind and one or two cards ahead on the record sheet.

ESP EVALUATION SCALE

Number of Runs (20 calls = 1 run)	Chance Score	ESP-Suggestive Score	ESP-Significant Score
5 runs	25 hits	34–35; or 15–16 hits	36 and over; or 14 or under hits
10 runs	50 hits	62–64; or 34–38 hits	65 and over; or 35 or under hits
15 runs	75 hits	90–92; or 58–60 hits	93 and over; or 57 or under hits

If after five runs you find your partner has scored 36 hits or over (on the nose or displaced), he has either cheated or used his psi powers to help him do it! A score of 34 or 35 is suggestive of this but not conclusive. Between 17 and 34 is chance expectation. If he has scored only 16, however, nine *under* chance expectation, he may well be using his ESP to help him *avoid* making correct guesses! If his score is 14 or below, this is even stronger evidence of negative psi.

Parapsychologists dub this phenomenon *psi missing:* using your psi power to help you tiptoe through the tulips, missing the targets. It crops up from time to time in the laboratory and often seems to be triggered by the subject's boredom, anger, discomfort, or even his skepticism. Of course, in a qualitative test it would read simply as a failure, but the quantitative approach shows up such sneaky uses of psi power in the same way an infrared photo shows up hidden heat sources. In an analysis made in 1972 of various personality types likely to exhibit psi missing in ESP tests, the following were listed:

tense	timid
excitable	shy
frustrated	withdrawn
demanding	submissive
impatient	suspicious
sensitive	depression-prone [7]

People showing these characteristics usually tend to suffer from varying degrees of anxiety. Anxiety is the very antithesis of that open state of mind characteristic of the well-adjusted, cheerful, responsive, adventuresome, self-assured psi-hitting type of person mentioned earlier. As we noted, our anxiety or openness may also be closely associated with the good or bad unconscious uses we put our psi to. Psychological openness itself, as we shall see later, is one of the psychological conditions we have to work toward to help us raise our ESP to an accessible level.

DECLINE EFFECT

Another thing you may notice in the pattern made by your scores is a general decline in the number of hits in the latter half, possibly followed by a sudden swoop up again right at the end. This frequently observed phenomenon is known as the *decline effect*. It is usually attributed to the subject's increasing lack of interest in the test, which is briefly stimulated again toward the end when the prospect of completion comes in sight.

STANDARD ESP CARD TESTS

If you feel like trying out your ESP on Standard ESP Cards, you can obtain a deck plus twenty-five printed record sheets from the Institute for Parapsychology, Box 6847, College Station, Durham, North Carolina 27708. They come with full instructions, so I will give only a general outline of their uses here. Various types of tests, each of which isolates a specific aspect of the ESP involved, can be performed with them. Personally, I find Standard ESP Cards work much better than regular playing cards for ESP tests. Whether it is the starkness of the symbols or their exciting associations with ESP that does this for me, I don't know. But I find I tend to get a higher percentage of correct guesses using them, although the "wavy lines" symbol never seems to come through so clearly as the other four. (See Figure 7.)

Figure 7. Standard ESP Card Symbols

GENERAL ESP (GESP) TESTS

Because of the difficulty of isolating telepathy in a test situation—you can never be sure that your psi has not clairvoyantly zeroed in on the card, rather than on the *thought* of the card—Rhine uses the term General ESP to describe this type of test. (Our test using regular playing cards fell into that category.)

Shuffle the twenty-five cards and have the sender turn one over and look at it. Only when he receives a signal to indicate the receiver has recorded his guess should he progress to the next. At the end of each run of twenty-five the guesses should be checked against the cards. (See Figure 8.) They may then be reshuffled for the next run. At least four runs should be completed for the statistics to take hold.

CLAIRVOYANCE TESTS (BT)

These are conducted in a similar manner to GESP tests, but the sender must refrain from looking at the card. He just picks the top card from the deck and places it face down on the table. Parapsychologists refer to this as BT, or Basic Test, procedure. You will note that precognitive telepathy could be an alternative explanation of above-chance scoring in all the clairvoyance tests.

CLAIRVOYANCE TESTS (DT)

DT stands for Down Through. Here the deck must be shuffled and left stacked for the receiver to use his ESP on, as is, without having them dealt out one by one. (I find I tend to get high forward displacement—one card ahead—scores by this method.)

MATCHING CLAIRVOYANCE TESTS

These are variants of the simple playing-card guessing test outlined earlier, using five cards showing the different ESP symbols from a *second* ESP deck to act as targets. (You will interfere with the statistics of evaluation if you remove them from the same deck.) These must be placed in five opaque manila envelopes, which are shuffled and laid out in a row before the subject. His task is to distribute the twenty-five cards of deck number one, without looking at their faces, in piles before each envelope, using his ESP to match the symbols. Again, he should not try to make the piles even.

EVALUATING YOUR SUCCESS

In using Standard ESP Cards, your success table, with five unknowns, is different from the earlier table, which is applicable to four. Again, check for forward and backward displacement, as this may be where you will find your highest scores.

ESP CARD TEST EVALUATION SCALE

Number of Runs (25 calls = 1 run)	Chance Score	ESP-Suggestive Score (odds 20 to 1)	ESP-Significant Score (odds 250 to 1)
4 runs	20 hits	28–31; or 9–12 hits	32 and over; or 8 or under hits
10 runs	50 hits	63–68; or 32–37 hits	69 and over; or 31 or under hits
50 runs	250 hits	279–292; or 208–231 hits	293 and over; or 207 or under hits
100 runs	500 hits	540–559; or 441–460 hits	560 and over; or 440 or under hits

ESP RECORD SHEET

No. __1.__

Subject __JOHN DOE__   Experiment __1.__

Observer __JANE DOE__   Date __9/19/74__

Type of Test __GESP (BT)__   Time __2.45 PM.__

General conditions __RELAXED - GOOD.__

Use other side for remarks.   Total score __10__   Avge. score __10__

With ESP cards use ∧ for star, o for circle, L for square, + for cross. = for waves.

1		2		3		4		5		6		7		8		9		10	
Call	Card	Call	Card	Call	Card	Call	Card	Call	Card	Call	Card	Call	Card	Call	Card	Call	Card	Call	Card
O	+																		
=	=																		
=	∧																		
∧	+																		
L	L																		
+	+																		
∧	∧																		
∧	o																		
+	=																		
=	+																		
+	o																		
O	O																		
L	L																		
∧	∧																		
O	O																		
=	o																		
+	+																		
O	+																		
L	+																		
=	L																		
=	L																		
O	=																		
∧	=																		
∧	∧																		
+	L																		
10																			

Figure 8. Standard ESP Card Record Sheet

TESTING YOUR ESP IN DREAMS

The occurrence of dreams that later turn out to be true or premonitory is a time-honored and legendary phenomenon. Quite apart from the wealth of anecdotal material concerning "true" dreams in psychoanalytic casebooks and the records of psychic research, experiments conducted in · the Menninger Dream Laboratory at Maimonides Medical Center, New York, over the past ten years provide overwhelming evidence, both quantitative and qualitative, that such dreams do in fact occur.[8] Dreaming quite apparently involves nonanalytical states of mind close to ideal for the emergence of ESP-scanned material. If you feel like prospecting your own dreams for veins of ESP scanning, here is a technique you can try. Like our picture-drawing experiment, it is a qualitative test.

Depending on the type of ESP you are going to try for, before going to sleep at night prepare for the test in one of the following ways. (Even if you wish simply to examine your dreams for significant signs of ESP, first try setting yourself one of these goals.)

YOUR GOAL

1. Concentrate your attention hard on a question you want answered, the more concrete the better, preferably something to which you can or will obtain the answer later (such as the outcome of an election). Write the question down one hundred times on a piece of paper and place it under your pillow. Or repeat it aloud one hundred times, thumping on your pillow once for each repetition. Make a little game out of it. (This always works best in ESP experiments.) Really give it all you've got to ram the question home.

2. Alternatively, get a friend to choose a colorful illustration from a book unknown to you and have him study it before he

goes to sleep. You, for your part, will try to sense in your dreams what the picture is. You must think hard about your friend and the picture before you fall asleep, asking yourself what the subject matter is, telling yourself you are going to find out tonight. You can also use the same technique of writing your question down or thumping it out.

REMEMBERING

When you awake, grab onto the first thought you have in your mind. Now use it as a thread to guide your memory back into your dreams. If you can remember your dreams without doing this, so much the better—not everybody can. Give about ten to twenty minutes to going over your dreams in your mind, jotting them down in a notebook. One dream may lead you back to others, for we rarely experience only one. But you will have to do this while they are still fresh in your mind. If you leave it until after breakfast, some of them will vanish beyond recall. Also note any words or phrases buzzing around in your head when you wake up, and any tunes or sounds too. Make a note of which dreams were particularly vivid, your reaction to them, whether you found them enjoyable or unpleasant and so on.

CHECKING FOR CLAIRVOYANCE AND TELEPATHY

When you get a moment during the day, survey your dream record and think about the images in your dream, particularly the people in it. If some are not immediately recognizable, ask yourself who of all the people you know they remind you of. What could the objects in the dreams signify? See if the question you asked has been answered in any way by the dream content, like an acted-out word charade. Even though the dream may simply be a repetition of something you have already experienced in the past, remember that a psi message is generally very economical and always employs your own memories and mental quirks to express itself.

If your friend has used a target picture, compare it with the dream. You may find you have acted out its subject matter or, alternatively, used it as scenery to back your dream play, building it out of things you have experienced yourself.

CHECKING FOR PRECOGNITION

During the days following, keep your eye on the news for any dramatic items that you think in some way parallel your dream. Note down any such strange coincidences beside the dream entry in your book. Also note parallel incidents that occur in your own life. Maybe you have already experienced the sudden realization that you have dreamed a current incident before. If you were lucky, you had told someone of the dream at the time, but this is generally the exception.

I recall one vivid dream I had that enacted itself in real life when I found myself on a totally unexpected trip to Ireland as a member of a documentary film crew. Unfortunately I hadn't told anyone about it when I had it several months previously. However, Christmas Day on top of the Rock of Cashel, with a westering sun and a crescent moon rising behind a Celtic stone cross in the east, is hardly your run-of-the-mill expectation. I don't think I had had much chance of consciously anticipating that one!

If you begin to find you have the knack of calling the shots on newsworthy items that make the press—particularly if they turn out to be accurate premonitions of catastrophic events—jot down any vivid dreams you feel might contain similar ESP warnings and send them to your local Premonitions Bureau.[9] This is a clearinghouse for potential ESP warnings. When a major disaster like the sinking of the *Titanic* looms in the future, several people sometimes receive ESP shadows of it in their dreams. Only recently, however, has there been any attempt to file and coordinate such precognitive dreams.

LUCID DREAMS

After keeping your dream diary for a while, you may find you are experiencing the occasional *lucid dream*—a dream in which for a moment you realize that you are dreaming. If the experience is a strong one, you may even remember who you are and what you did in waking life the day before. People who have experienced lucid dreaming find a radical change occurs in their dream life: Instead of remaining helpless players in an uncontrollable drama, they find themselves able to take an active part in the dream, experimenting with the situations by which they find themselves confronted.[10]

Although an extraordinary and little-understood psychological phenomenon, lucid dreaming itself does not seem to relate to psi, although a further state of consciousness often reached via the lucid dream does: the out-of-the-body experience (usually abbreviated to OOBE or simply OBE). Astral projection, as it used to be called, is a phenomenon long attested to in the records of psychic research. In fact, along with telepathy and mediumship, astral projection was one of the chief interests of the founding fathers of the original Society for Psychical Research in England. Indeed, the out-of-the-body experience may well turn out to be the most significant psi phenomenon of all. We shall accordingly be returning to it later in greater detail, for it really deserves a chapter to itself.

FOUR

Developing Your ESP

Today the emphasis in parapsychology seems to be shifting away from "Does psi exist?" to the question of "How does it work?" Most researchers appear to have accepted the evidence for its existence. The next step is to learn how to turn it on and off at will, to produce it in the laboratory. This is easier said than done.

Very few people, it seems, possess the natural ability to make conscious use of their psi. Most of us just seem to have a basic psi-scanning ability, and that's about the extent of it. Unlike born psychics, we lack the means of objectifying our ESP signals and so becoming aware of them.

INFORMATION-FEEDBACK LEARNING

The problem of learning how to use one's psi is, of course, closely related to the question of what exactly takes place inside our heads when it occurs. If we can shed light on the one, it will probably help us to come to grips with the other.

Parapsychologists today are using electronic guessing machines, sophisticated versions of Tyrrell's clairvoyance testing gadget, to provide subjects with information feedback about their ESP—instant knowledge of correct or incorrect guesses. In this way they hope to teach them to start identifying any telltale body or psychological sensations that might accompany accurate psi-mediated guesses. If you make an appointment to visit the ASPR laboratory in New York, you can try out your own skill in this type of psychic bingo. Their "Espateacher" machine, designed in 1966 by Dr. Charles Tart, is on loan to them from the University of Virginia Medical School.

ESP AND THE EEG

Another popular ESP feedback-learning tool is the electroencephalograph (EEG), a device that measures and records the electrical currents given off by the nerves of the brain. Wires attached to the scalp of the subject relay the minute electrical brain currents to an amplifier and thence to an oscilloscope or a trace recorder. Here they are reproduced visually for analysis. The currents pulse in a variety of rhythms of between 0.5 and 30 cycles per second, and these rhythmic patterns indicate the type of activity going on in the brain. Slow, regular rhythms are characteristic of a state of unconsciousness in the subject. During waking consciousness they become fretted by faster, irregular pulses.

Four basic types of rhythm are considered to be representative of four different states of consciousness: "beta" rhythms, fast pulses of 13 to 30 cycles per second, characteristic of attention and alert concentration; "alpha" rhythms of 8 to 13 cycles, characteristic of a state of poised relaxation; "theta" rhythms of 4 to 8 cycles, characteristic of drowsiness, dreaming and creative imagination; and lastly "delta" rhythms, slow, regular pulses of 0.5 to 4 cycles per second, characteristic of deep, dreamless sleep. We spend our lives moving up and down this electrical spectrum as our state of consciousness alters from one moment to the next.

ESP subjects tested with the electroencephalograph have been observed to demonstrate ascending alpha rhythms while they are making accurate guesses indicative of ESP.[1] We can view this observation alongside statements made by various psychics past and present to the effect that ESP requires a special blankness of mind to allow the impression to surface. This may be a way of describing the poised relaxation characteristic of the alpha rhythm. Knowing what we do about the ESP transaction taking place beneath our threshold of consciousness, it is not hard to understand why the alpha rhythm should be favorable to ESP, indicating as it does a kind of watershed between consciousness and unconsciousness. Its observed acceleration may be due to the increase of the subject's attention as he focuses on the task of discovering the target.

The ESP process, by all accounts, seems a little like fishing in a pool to retrieve a lost object: the pool being our own unconscious brain processes, the lost object the ESP signal, the line our focused attention. After a period of latency, up comes the object entangled in pond weed—various symbolically associated fears, wishes or memories that the ESP signal has hooked onto, or may in fact be expressing itself in. Like clothing giving form to the Invisible Man, ESP signals appear to borrow our subconscious material—half-forgotten memories, associations, fantasies or fears—using the relevant ones to express themselves in our consciousness. Looked at from another point of view, ESP signals may be said to jog our subconscious memories by stimulating already existing neural pathways in our brains. These memories become the impressions that we compare with the target material to see if we have had an ESP experience. The task of the sensitive, then, may well be threefold: He must relax his analytical processes to allow his normally unconscious memory pool to become accessible; then he must send out an ESP probe or line to hook the most applicable memory from the pool; then he must net the catch.

TRANCE MEDIUMSHIP

Various techniques have been evolved down the ages that seem to enable sensitives to do these things. The trance state cultivated by primitive shamans and later by spiritualist mediums is probably the oldest. Here the sensitive is taught, or teaches himself, by a process of suggestion or autosuggestion to set aside temporarily the everyday, analytical part of his mind. If he is so prone, the gap may then be filled by another, hidden, facet of his personality, often a fragmentary secondary personality, which in spiritualistic circles is considered to be a possessing spirit on account of the apparently supernormal information it may impart.

A closely related type of trance was also favored by the nineteenth-century mediums known as somnambulists: the so-called mesmeric trance, a hypnotic variety in which the subject temporarily places the controls of his personality in the hands of another person, the hypnotist. The trance itself, however, does not appear to be an integral part of the ESP process. Sensitives trained in the techniques of spiritualism, like Eileen Garrett, have found that they can discard trance altogether once they have learned from it the knack of ESP "fishing." The trance would then seem to be a psychological prop, possibly a device for focusing the attention inward and shifting anxiety-causing responsibility for the phenomena that are (or are not) about to be demonstrated onto the shoulders of the secondary personality or hypnotist.

Interestingly enough, it has long been observed by psychic researchers that one of the major obstacles in trying to cultivate one's psi faculty is one's own skepticism. Nothing produces psi missing quicker than disbelief. Practicing psychics seem to cope with this generally very healthy mental trait by working out rationales for themselves, theories that account for their ESP and, temporarily at least, take care of their disruptive skepticism. Psi rationales can run the gamut from Divine Grace through spirit entities to force fields. Of course a rationale may turn out to be true in the end, but from the psychic's point of view of psi production, this is almost beside the issue. The spiritualist credo undoubtedly provides such a comfortable rationale. But playing around with trances and deliberate mental dissociation involved in mediumism obviously has its risks. The mind is a delicate mechanism, and the dangers involved in courting artificially induced schizophrenia, which is what trance personalities could be termed, are surely apparent.

Automatic writing, the ability some people have to write unconsciously composed scripts, is another type of trance phenomenon. Some of the most persuasive evidence of psi scanning was produced early in this century in the form of automatic scripts written independently by mediums ignorant of the existence of one another. So remarkably did these automatically written texts interlock—one frequently took up where the other left off, or supplied the key to another's previously given cryptic utterance—that a number of prominent parapsychologists to this day consider the "Cross correspondences," as they have come to be known in the literature of psi, to be important evidence for the postmortem survival of the personalities allegedly dictating them through the mediums.[2] Whether or not the scripts were prompted by spirits or the mediums' own psi powers is still debated. That they were produced by the unconscious movement of people's hands is surely a most amazing thing, spirits or no.

ESP BY AUTOMATISMS

Body movements that occur without the conscious control of the person experiencing them are known as motor automatisms. While automatic writing, which falls under this heading, is always overshadowed by the built-in risks of involuntary schizophrenia, there exist other, more rudimentary, types of automatism that seem to avoid them. These are the easiest types of fishing lines to the unconscious that one can use, and they have been employed as such at least since the Middle Ages and probably before.

If you have ever experienced a nerve twitching in your eyelid or found your hand shaking after carrying a heavy suitcase around for a while, then you have experienced an unconscious motor automatism. It was unconscious because, as you probably found out, there was not much you could do to control it while it lasted. "Butterflies in the stomach" experienced before an important interview is another type of unconscious automatism.

Many gifted psychics have discovered that their intuition first comes to them via such common automatisms as "butter-flies" or a "feeling in my bones" or even "prickling of my thumbs." Recent experiments indicate that the rise and fall of blood pressure can also be triggered by an unfelt ESP signal.[3] Such psi-mediated responses are usually vague and seem to serve mainly as signals alerting the sensitive to inquire within for further information, rather like the mailman ringing the bell to let you know he has delivered a package.

One of the easiest types of motor-automatism pegs we can hang our psi on is one originating in our hand and arm. We can render the automatism visible by means of a pendulum, at its simplest just a ring or key hung on a twelve-inch piece of string. Such a device is frequently used by dowsers for locating springs of fresh water or lost objects.

HOW TO USE A PENDULUM

Any type of small weight attached to a string will do as your pendulum. Dowsers often use elaborate hollow "doodlebugs," as they are known in the trade, which they fill with a sample of the type of substance they are prospecting for—water, oil or mineral ore. For our purposes, however, a key or heavy ring will be sufficient. (See Figure 9.) Hold the end of the string in one hand and dangle it away from your body. After a minute or two your hand will begin to move with the strain. Allow it to do so. The movement will communicate itself to the pendulum, which will soon start swinging to and fro in various directions. There is nothing paranormal about any of this so far. You are simply demonstrating unconscious muscular spasms.

Now we must establish a code so we can "communicate" with our pendulum. If you think about it a moment, you will see that there are basically three distinct types of movement our pendulum can perform:

1. It can swing from side to side.

2. It can swing backward and forward.

3. It can start swinging around in a circle.

Draw a six- to nine-inch-diameter circle on a piece of paper and divide it into quarters with two lines through the center.

Now seat yourself in a chair and place the paper on the floor before you. Take the pendulum in your hand and let it dangle so the weight is hanging approximately over the intersecting lines. After a minute your hand will begin to move from muscle strain and the pendulum will sway. Out loud, treating it as an independent entity, ask it to signify the word "yes" to you and watch for the rhythm it adopts. If it goes around in a circle, write YES on the circumference of your chart. YES will be a circular motion in *your* code. If it swings from side to side, or backward and forward, write YES on the appropriate line. Now ask it to

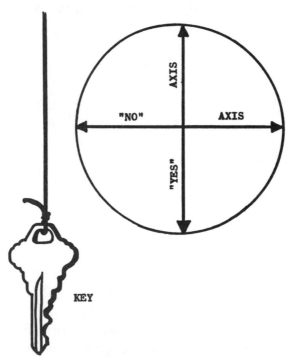

Figure 9. Pendulum and Chart

signify "no" to you, again noting the result down on the chart. If "yes" was a back-and-forth swing, "no" may be shown as a side-to-side or circular motion.

Once you have established your code, you can go on to test your pendulum's "knowledge" by asking it questions to which you yourself do not know the answer but which someone else in the room does. Or get someone to hide a coin under one of three cups and try to make your pendulum tell you which one it lies under with a "yes" sign. To get the pendulum to signify numbers or letters, dangle it in a wide tumbler or small bowl and count the number of times it strikes against the side. Try to get it to tell the time in this way. Of course in a test like this we have no guarantee that ESP is responsible for any correct answers we get. However, if we consistently go on getting correct answers, we can reasonably conclude that our involuntary muscle movements are being prompted by unconscious knowledge, possibly derived via psi.

At this point, you may like to try your hand at map dowsing. Draw a rough plan of your house on a large piece of paper and get someone to hide an object somewhere in one of the rooms. Now, instead of physically going to explore the rooms with your pendulum, hang it over the plan and see if you can get a "yes" response over any room in particular. Then, out loud, call off the likely spots where the object might be hidden and see how the pendulum responds. If you cannot get a clear reading by this method, go to the room indicated and proceed as you would in the cup test, using your pendulum to explore likely hiding places.

Needless to say, not everyone can get consistently good results with a pendulum. I cannot, for one, although I've met people who claim they can. My uncle can use a forked twig to find water in much the same way, but the talent has passed me by. Maybe I'm too analytical a person to allow my unconscious motor reflexes to really get going.[4] But where one can fail, many can sometimes succeed.

GROUP AUTOMATISM METHODS

For people like myself group automatism will frequently work while solo methods will not. Whether this is because one has other people present to whom one can unconsciously throw the responsibility, I don't know. It's a possibility, at any rate.

TABLE TILTING

The easiest form of group automatism to perform is so-called table tilting. A relic from the days of nine-teenth-century spiritualism, it has lingered on among nonspirit-ualists as a party game.

Any number can play, the more the merrier. The table should be round, light, without casters and resting on a hard floor. Each seated person's hands should be placed lightly on the top, thumbs touching and little fingers meeting those of his neighbor. After a time ranging from five to twenty minutes the table will begin to move. The weird feeling it gives you as it begins to twist and scrape about under your hands has to be experienced to be believed, even though you know the cause to be your own collective unconscious reflexes. After the first few twistings and turnings it should begin to tilt backward and forward on two of its legs. At this point you can inform it of your code: one tap for "yes," two taps for "no." Treat the table as an entity as you did the pendulum, taking turns in asking it questions. When dates or ages are required, count the number of taps. Names may be spelled out by going deliberately through the alphabet, each tap standing for a letter. The letter where the table misses a beat is the relevant one.

Again, as with the pendulum, the percentage of psi-guided responses is hard to gauge. However, if you get a good group together, the information you can elicit by this means can be extraordinary and fascinating.

A less laborious method of using group automatism to spell

out information is by means of the Ouija board or its simpler relation, the glass game.

THE GLASS GAME

Again, any number can take part. Lay out the letters of the alphabet—write them on small pieces of paper or use Scrabble tiles—in a circle on a smooth tabletop, leaving at least an inch or two between them. On opposite sides of the circle place the written words YES and NO. Now place a broad-mouthed but lightweight glass tumbler upside down in the center of the circle. Each member of the company should rest a finger lightly on the upended bottom of the glass. After a short period of time, your glass will begin to slide around, slowly at first, picking up speed, circling and darting from letter to letter, spelling out phrases and words. As in table tilting, take turns in asking it questions. Again, the movement is caused by the combined unconscious muscular reactions of everyone present. However, the information derived from the game can be just as mystifyingly accurate as any received from a high-scoring psychic. If paranormal in origin, it would appear to derive from the collective psi talents of your group, or alternatively that of one or two of the members transmitted via involuntary and imperceptible nervous impulses in their fingers.

OTHER ESP CHANNELS

Not everyone's ESP chooses automatism to show itself. The hunch, dream or meaningful coincidence seems to be an even more common channel. Is there any way, one wonders, that we might turn these to account; that is, artificially induce ESP-guided hunches, dreams or meaningful coincidences?

ESP "BROADCASTING"

Dr. Milan Ryzl, a well-known Czechoslovakian parapsychologist whose recent work in the field of hypnotic ESP induction has uncovered Pavel Stepanek, one of the most reliably high-scoring psychics known today, proposes the following formula for deliberate ESP production:

1. Send out an intensive questioning thought about the target.

2. Make your mind a blank and wait for the answer to rise into consciousness.[5]

Dr. Ryzl suggests that *all* conscious thought produces waves of psi energy. The more intense the thought, the bigger the burst of energy. Likewise, the more prolonged the thought, or series of similar thoughts, the greater the output of psi. Pursuing our radar analogy of Chapter Two, let us say our psi wave radiates from our vicinity and interacts with the psi fields of other people or objects. If our psi wave now returns to us *modified* by the pattern of the psi field of the object or person it came in contact with and proceeds to stimulate relevant circuits in our own brain (now acting as a receiver), we will say we have received a telepathic or clairvoyant impression. If on the other hand our psi wave modifies or alters in some way the pattern of the psi field of the person it comes in contact with, *he* will say he has received a telepathic flash. You would, in effect, have projected your thought into his mind.

This is all, of course, highly speculative and hypothetical, but, interestingly enough, Dr. Ryzl seems to be describing something in theoretical terms that may have been practiced in a quite matter-of-fact way in Europe over four hundred years ago. (What I'm going to propose now will probably make most parapsychologists cringe, so before I proceed any further let me make it clear that this next section is not parapsychology, although the principles involved may turn out to be parapsychological.)

In his book on cryptography and methods of sending secret messages, the fifteenth-century occult philosopher and abbot of Spanheim, Johannes Trithemius, claimed to have perfected a means of mentally communicating thoughts over a distance "without superstition or the aid of spirits." Not only could his method do this, he claimed, but it could also be used to obtain knowledge "of everything that is happening in the world." [6] Trithemius was backed up in his extravagant claim by his pupil Henry Cornelius Agrippa, who wrote of his own experiments in this direction:

It is possible, naturally, without any kind of superstition, and through the mediation of no other spirit, for a man to convey his thoughts to someone else in a very short time, however far apart they may be from each other; and though the time in which this is done cannot be exactly measured, it will inevitably happen within twenty-four hours. And I know how to do this and have often done it. Abbot Trithemius also knew how to do it and used to do it. [7]

The process Trithemius used for his telepathic telephone was a complex one. It involved working out pages of elaborate astrological calculations to find the correct hour to send the message, at which time one repeated the spoken message over two drawings, one a sketch of the recipient and the other a naked, bearded man standing on a multicolored bull and holding a pen in his left hand, a book in his right. This was supposed to represent Orifiel, the angel thought to be in charge of this type of experiment. These images then had to be buried under a threshold, a time-honored witchy practice. The message would be conveyed within a day, or alternatively, depending on your intention, you would learn what you wished to know about the recipient in that space of time. Or so Trithemius said.

Now, discounting the medieval mumbo jumbo and astrology and reducing Trithemius's method into its basic terms, we see that he is simply advocating two things:

1. A long period of sustained concentration (the astrological calculations) with the thought of the person you are inquiring about continuously at the back of your mind.

2. An abrupt dismissal of the thought, characterized by burying the two pictures in the ground.

Of course it is more than just possible that Trithemius and Agrippa were deluding themselves, or simply lying through their teeth. But it is interesting to note the similarity between their formula and Dr. Ryzl's: the intensive mental probe followed by the blanking of the mind or, in Trithemius's case, putting the subject out of the mind.

Is there any other evidence that sustained concentration of thought can produce paranormal "answers" in this way? Well, we have the time-honored practice of prayer. The early Church certainly considered it productive of meaningful coincidences, be they in the form of relevant passages of Scripture conveniently coming to one's attention or more impressive dreams or external "signs and portents." Maybe their "working of the Holy Spirit" was simply psi expressed in religious terms. Can we, then, bearing all these intriguing hints in mind, somehow boil them down into a simple, testable method for producing "answers" psychically? I believe we can.

Let's say, for the sake of argument, you decide to try to send a telepathic message to a close friend or relative far away. One of the easiest ways you can do this, without even being aware of it, is simply by writing him a long letter. If your *motivation* for writing the letter has been strong enough and your emotional link with him sufficiently great, you may well find, rather irritatingly, that your letter crosses one from him asking all the questions you supplied the answers for or, alternatively, supplying the answers for all your questions! I am sure we have all experienced this type of phenomenon, and I believe its explanation lies in the psi-scanning process again focused by emotive concentration.

Can we do this deliberately? Next time, as an experiment, try writing a letter and *not* posting it, and see what happens. You will have to make sure that while you write it you behave as you normally would when writing a regular letter: mentally addressing it to the recipient as if you were in his presence, and so on. The letter must be as "alive" as a regular one. Choose as your recipient someone with whom you have a close emotional bond. Give enough time for an answering letter to arrive before taking the initiative and checking with your friend as to whether or not he felt impelled to write. Keep in mind, however, that an

ESP message is only one of the many unconscious promptings that we weigh in the balance before taking any action. Theoretically, it is quite possible for an ESP signal to get through but simply be overlooked by the receiver because other considerations were stronger, such as lack of time, energy or opportunity.

On another tack, if you wish to give your directed psi-scanning process a clairvoyant task, write a short, repetitive essay asking *yourself* the questions you want answered; then hide it and forget about it. Obviously, you aren't going to get a phone call or letter from yourself in response to this type of experiment (at least I hope not), but you may start finding meaningful coincidences relevant to your question starting to crop up soon after. How soon seems to vary. Sometimes I have found it happening the very next day; at other times six months have passed before I've gotten a "reply."

A spontaneous example of this type of psi scanning occurred to me only this morning. I had spent half of it searching hard and in vain for a description of a piece of sailing gear known as a bosun's chair, which I needed for a television movie script I am writing. I picked up a magazine that is sent to me gratis by a credit card company, and after remarking what a waste of money I think their sending it to me is, I flipped it open—I usually toss it straight in the trash—and, you've guessed it, there was a color photograph of a bosun's chair.

If anything other than chance is at work here, let me emphasize again I believe it to be a perfectly natural principle: my own psi field bringing relevant information to my attention, leading me unconsciously toward it, perhaps even leading it to me.

Writing "letters," of course, is only one of many ways of concentrating our attention in the right way for a psi task. During the Middle Ages Cabalists evolved another variant. They were Jewish mystics who combined the practice of contemplation with the study of the text of the Hebrew Scripture for coded spiritual meanings. They also made a practice of writing their prayers down, reducing them to their component letters and then performing mental gymnastics with these letters as a form of meditative exercise.[8] Sometimes the letters were written down in the form of acrostics, and the resultant squares were kept as amulets believed to draw the desired information or situations to their keepers.

Still another medieval method for sending out forceful prayers—this one very common among people who could neither read nor write—was simply to tie knots in a piece of string or hide, repeating the intention again and again over each knot. This, of course, is only an early, witchy version of telling the beads of a rosary.

All these methods, once you strip away their romance and occultism, seem initially to have one thing in common: concentrating the attention in order to make use of one's natural ESP-scanning ability. It is far easier to do this if one involves oneself in a mental game of some sort, if one psychs oneself, whether by tying knots in a piece of string, drawing pictures or diagrams of one's goal, writing it down on a piece of paper or even acting it out as a symbolic charade or "happening" like the one Drs. Krippner, Ullman and Honorton used for their precognition experiment.[9] The two points to remember with this type of experiment seem to be:

1. A period of total, committed, concentrated attention to send out the psi signal.

2. Putting the matter completely out of one's mind.

Interestingly enough, I find that the Swedish sensitive Olof Jonsson proposes what in effect is really a simplified example of this method. He advocates the following experiment:

1. Erase all thoughts from your mind.

2. Relax your body.

3. Visualize an object that you would like to buy for your wife.

4. Concentrate for a few moments on it, then forget about it. Jonsson stresses the importance of forgetting, lest you "draw the thought back to you."

5. When you get home, check the efficacy of your

broadcasting by asking your wife what present she would like you to buy for her.[10]

ESP VISION

I suppose one might almost call the method I am about to describe next the Professional's Method of ESP. Scrying, lucidity, clairvoyance are some of the many terms by which this technique has been known down the years. Although shrouded in mystery and romance, the method itself rests upon a perfectly natural ability we all possess to produce pictures in our mind's eye. There is nothing supernormal about it, although it can begin to seem so if the pictures start conforming to an outward reality.

If you try staring for a while at an old stain on a plaster wall as Leonardo da Vinci once did, this picture-making faculty of your mind will probably begin organizing it into an image of something familiar like a profile or a tree or a landscape. Psychologists make use of our tendency to do this in the Rorschach test—a series of inkblot shapes made by folding a blob of ink into a piece of paper—into which the patient reads associated ideas that are then analyzed for their emotional content. Like any automatism, this image-making faculty of our mind can be used as a peg on which to hang our ESP impression. This may be what fortune-tellers do when they read the pattern of the tea leaves in a cup or the drippings of a candle in water.

Our mental picture-making faculty lies fallow in most of us. Little children and primitive peoples possess it in a far higher degree, but it seems to fade away when they start thinking analytically. I recall that I myself retained the ability to close my eyes and watch the "pictures" within my head until I was about six or seven years old, but I had to work quite hard to get it back again later. I used to be able to see things even by looking at a patch of dark color or any dark opening. Sensitives who employ this method of fishing in the unconscious sometimes use a small screen or tray covered with black velvet, or even a black mirror.

When I talked to him about it, Gerard Croiset referred to the vision itself as a "window" that appears to him in the air. Now that I consider it, I think perhaps what one does in "vision" is to use the regular visual neural pathways of the brain on their own but allow them to freewheel, as it were, without an external stimulus.

If you feel like trying to develop your ESP in this direction, then your best course is to start relearning how to see these mental pictures as I did. Don't bother with black screens and psychic gadgets for the time being. Simply close your eyes in a darkened room. The ideal time to do this, I find, is before falling asleep at night, but not when you are overtired. You must be able to focus your attention, and fatigue precludes this.

These, approximately, are the steps you may follow. They may well be unique to me, but I give them for what they are worth as personal observations:

1. Close your eyes and look into the darkness of your eyelids.

2. Allow your thought processes to die down while still maintaining your "looking" attitude all the while. You may observe odd little shapes go floating across your field of vision from time to time, sometimes singly, sometimes joined in branchy clumps of two or three. Don't get excited about these, however. They are blood corpuscles in your eye, not psychic impressions.

3. After a while—anything from two to twenty minutes—you may notice what I in my childish vernacular used to call a "shaking" appear in the inner darkness. This is a net or weblike structure stretched across part or all of one's field of vision, which begins to shake, slowly at first, then faster. In my experience, shakings always precede the pictures. I suppose the pictures evolve out of the shaking itself.

(Of course you may not find you experience this type of primary image. Eileen Garrett's appears to have been a shape like a yew tree that would split in two, bend over and turn itself into various shapes out of which the other images would appear.[11] Other sensitives see moving foliage or intricate light patterns.)

4. When the primary image dies down, you may get your first sense of depth, a feeling that you are staring into three-dimensional space. In this depth the "imaginals" (as I named them) appear, dimly at first, but more solidly and clearly with practice. These may be things you know in daily life like books or bottles or flowers, or they may be large abstract shapes, often architectural in appearance. Keep your mental gaze on them and you'll notice that they all seem to be in motion, drifting about like fish in an aquarium, in and out of your field of vision. You will also notice that they are all continually growing and evolving into something else, like a speeded-up film of a plant growing. When I saw my first surrealist painting as a child, I knew exactly what the artist was portraying.

If you work away at this ability, in time you can bring it to a point where you can employ it in full daylight, using a black background on which to project your images, or simply by closing your eyes and holding your hands over them. Incidentally, it's fun to experiment with this type of looking on sleepless nights or when you are sick in bed with a cold, and certainly it is one way of bypassing the customary feeling of uselessness one experiences on such occasions.

But this is only two-thirds of the battle. You are not truly clairvoyant yet. Your visions are haphazard ones. You have a screen on which you can project images from your unconscious mind—or, to use our familiar analogy, it is your fishing line to your unconscious memory pool—but you still have to hook the correct impression by making the connection with the goal, your ESP target.

This seems to be accomplished chiefly by the strength of your intention, your motivation, your genuine desire to see or find out. It is something we shall be studying in greater detail in the next chapter.

FIVE

Using Your ESP

Our vision technique gives us access to an unconscious reservoir of potential ESP impressions, but we still have to learn the knack of hooking the right one, in preference to any of the other teeming images. The means of doing this is simple—or it seems so at first glance. It can be summed up in one word: motivation. One has to be genuinely interested in making the contact, and this, like most things that require getting your mind to play ball with you, is often easier said than done.

As we noted previously, people who do well at producing ESP often possess open, outgoing, interested and gregarious personalities. They also tend toward generalization in their thinking processes rather than analytical thought. Often they are generous and all-embracing in their appraisal of things, rather than critical. In a word, they are childlike, though not necessarily childish.[1]

Creative people also seem to be open to greater degrees of ESP than analytical, noncreative types. This may have something to do with their being more in touch with their reservoir of unconscious images and more open to spontaneous behavior. Boredom, skepticism, rigidity of behavior, doubt, pain and anxiety are all fatal to conscious ESP. They seem to scramble the signals and often not only cause the sensitive to produce random results but even start him on a psi-missing jag. Basil Shackleton moaned about the suffocating boredom of endless statistical testing with ESP cards, and Eileen Garrett complained that ESP cards did not live or radiate for her, that they did not express an emotion. She claimed that this sterility forced her to reach telepathically for the emotions of the person who was handling the cards rather than clairvoyantly to survey the cards themselves.[2]

Noticing this importance of stimulus and motivation, researchers have tried introducing stimulating subject matter as target material rather than the customary stars and circles, and in so doing obtained significantly higher results. For instance, when pictures showing nude men and women engaged in sexual activities were used as ESP targets, subjects normally disturbed by graphic portrayals of such subjects tended to show high psi missing of the targets, whereas those without such inhibitions scored higher positively.[3]

Because of the importance, then, of motivation—the reasons that compel one to make the ESP contact—many budding sensitives seem to find it far easier to develop their psi by working with people rather than cards as targets. If they happen to be naturally nosy about other people's affairs, so much the better. If you belong to this group, here is one approach to the technique you can try.

PEOPLE READING

Your goal in this experiment is to sense an object that your target person has concealed on himself. You may find you have not perceived this and have focused on something completely different about the target person, but the object serves as an aim to start out with. There are four effective hooks you can use to motivate this type of personal ESP contact:

1. Admiration. The target person is worthy of your respect. By demonstrating your ESP to him you will earn his respect. Many sensitives are motivated by their desire to impress or please their client or the parapsychologist who is testing them.

2. Sexual attraction. The target person is sexually interesting to you. Many of the greatest mediums, such as Eusapia Palladino, seem to have performed best when "turned on" by their sitters.

3. Compassion. The target person is suffering from some traumatic problem or emotional conflict with which you can identify, either through a similar experience of your own or through one of someone close to you: a lost child or relative, the physical danger of someone dear to him or her, the solution of a theft or such.

4. Winning. By demonstrating your ESP, something you deeply want or need will become yours, whether it be simply prestige or some type of prize. (This type of motivation is not always reliable, however. It can produce nullifying anxiety about the prospect of failure rather than a positive stimulus. Not everyone rises to a challenge in the same way. I personally have found it impossible to produce any type of ESP for a material reward.)

YOUR ESP PROCEDURE

In 1964 Rhea White completed a survey of various sensitives' observations about the way they obtained their ESP impressions, and found a considerable similarity among them.[4] She isolated five distinct steps that seemed to be integral to all the methods:

1. Physical relaxation. Most sensitives agree on the necessity of this condition.

2. The demand or intention to pick up an ESP impression. This seems to be another way of describing the focusing of attention needed for the ESP task. Maybe it is the subjective equivalent of our "psi probe."

3. Stilling the conscious mind, by whatever means.

4. A period of deliberate waiting, accompanied by a

mounting tension, releasable only by the advent of an impression.

5. Some means by which the impression can enter the sensitive's consciousness, such as by way of a hunch, vision, voice, automatism or unconsciously motivated doodle that starts a chain of other impressions.

Spelled out, then, here is the procedure for ESP production as given by White and filled out with personal observations and those of other sensitives like Eileen Garrett.

PRELIMINARY PREPARATIONS

Choose a quiet room with not too strong lighting. The person you are going to "read" should not inhibit you unduly nor be an extreme skeptic, since we know that strong negative emotions seem to scramble the ESP signals. However, this does not mean you should exclude strangers. Many find they can work better with them than with friends, as they offer a challenge to their curiosity.

Make sure you are neither tired nor anxious, but relaxed and mentally alert, as though you were sitting down to some entertaining parlor game. A cup of tea or coffee often helps to produce the right ESP mood. Explain to your target person that you are not trying for clairvoyance or precognition, merely general ESP. Keep the atmosphere informal and have someone on hand with a pencil and paper to jot down your impressions as you speak them. Better still, use a tape recorder, provided it does not inhibit you. Choose a comfortable armchair for yourself.

Step 1 RELAXATION

Make sure you're quite relaxed before you begin. Many sensitives use deep breathing to loosen up the tense stomach muscles here. Eileen Garrett found that a few really deep breaths at the beginning of each session helped her to focus her attention as well as to compel the muscles of her abdomen to relax. "From that moment, any question of error and insecurity of interpretation is over," she wrote.[5]

If you wish to use Progressive Relaxation exercises to help you relax, go ahead and use them. (See Appendix I.) I myself find just having a good stretch is usually sufficient.

Step 2 THE DEMAND

Now we come to the motivational part. Rhea White's "demand" seems to be the psychological equivalent of our hypothetical ESP probe. Eileen Garrett says of it: "All the perceptions are quickened, and it seems as though hearing, seeing, sensing and knowing have tied themselves to a white beam which is sent hither and thither as the will calls it to obey."[6] Elsewhere she calls it, rather more simply, "alert expectation."[7] Another sensitive known to Mrs. Garrett referred to this state as making yourself one with the subject, knowing that consciousness is one. This is, in fact, where your emotional bond plays its part in linking you with your target person. I also find it helpful here to make a deliberate mental observation to myself that my psi-scanning process is *going on all the time*, whether I will it or no, and that my task is simply to direct my attention to the subject and read the signals that my psi field is *already* receiving.

Then really zero in on the subject. If he is holding a concealed target for you to sense, tell yourself that you *already* know what it is but merely have to find out from yourself. Try to do this attention fixing in a spirit of "high carelessness," another Garrett phrase, not grim determination. Try to give it a buoyancy that literally elevates you psychologically, like the glow you used to get when you were about to start a race you knew you stood a good chance of winning or an examination that you were going to excel at. "I can and, what's more, I will!" or even the show-off's "Look at me, I can fly!" must be your attitude here. It feels a bit like holding your breath and standing poised on tiptoe.

Step 3 STILLING THE CONSCIOUS MIND

Having sent out our ESP probe toward the target, we must now put our minds into a condition to receive the returning echo, to pursue our radar analogy. This echo, when it comes, will be couched in symbols plucked from our own subconscious memories and perceived by our vision technique.

Push aside your thinking processes here. Shut off the garbled internal commentary too. Push it away and ignore it. "The emotional process for reception is pure placidity," wrote Mrs. Garrett. "I see myself as plastic, empty, at perfect rest. I have nothing to do except automatically to describe what is appearing before my inner vision." [8]

Step 4 WAITING

Close your eyes and look, using your vision technique. If you prefer, hold your palms over your eyes and keep them open, staring into the darkness made by your hands. Some sensitives find they can start the image flow quickly by turning their eyes upward in their heads.

Step 5 MEANS BY WHICH THE IMPRESSION CAN ENTER THE CONSCIOUSNESS

If you find the image flow slow in starting, take your pencil and paper and start doodling. Then close your eyes and use the images stirred up by the doodles as a starting point. It has been a matter of frequent observation that ESP-mediated images seem to appear at the moment when the *conscious attention is distracted* in some way. It may well be that the actual ESP signal is hooked during the gap between demand and reception.

Warcollier's latency and the phenomenon of displacement may in fact turn out to be a much more integral part of the ESP process than mere time-lag effects. By recording a card in an ESP test, we may well "clear a space" for the ESP signal of the fore or after card to fill. Therefore the need to switch off one's conscious attention at this stage is probably a very real one. By watching our own interior movie show we can very effectively combine both necessities: 1) the need for distraction, and 2) the need for a "fishing line." Doodling is a good way of "clearing an empty space" quickly.

Watch the patterns move, and wait for recognizable objects to form on your inner screen. Do not rush them or yourself. You may have to wait fifteen minutes or longer. Allow yourself plenty of time. Pretend your field of vision is a smooth, unruffled lake. Allow yourself not to care what happens, as though you were in a state of careless daydreaming. Teach yourself to forget about your original intention. Simply keep watching idly, as you did in your initial visioning. "The clairvoyant image 'happens.' You come upon it. It might always have been there.... You have done nothing ... except look within where the image is enthroned," says Eileen Garrett.[9] Accept the images for what they are. Don't try to guess at their meanings yet. As you get more proficient you may begin to see recurring images and realize that, like dream symbols, they carry a special personal meaning for you. But this only comes with practice. Just wait for the images to solidify, then blurt them out, however clumsy your description sounds. If a black square appears, *say* a black square. If you get the feeling it's a black swimming pool, say you have a *feeling* it's a black swimming pool, not that you *see* one. In all probability your everyday analytical mind will not know what the image means at first, but your target person may. If any stray phrases or words start running through your head for no apparent reason, blurt them out too. I remember one ESP dream experiment I tried using a regular afternoon nap as my "fishing line." I dreamed I heard a voice singing the words of Ariel's "Sea Song" from Shakespeare's *The Tempest*: "Full fathom five thy father lies," and so on. My target person, I learned later, was preparing a lecture on *The Tempest*.

SIGNS OF ACCURACY

When it comes to the crunch, each sensitive evolves his own way of recognizing which picture is the accurate one. This is particularly relevant when there is a specific target object to sense. I personally find that accuracy seems to be indicated by those images that are persistent; that is, which resist the usual melting process or keep recurring. Some sensitives, however, find that the correct images are those they recognize first, others those that appear in color or those accompanied by a feeling of rightness or exhilaration. If you try the instant information-feedback approach and get your target person to confirm the accuracy of the images as you blurt them out, you may discover that the correct image has a special feeling or attribute other than any of the above.

ESP COUNSELING

If you do experiment with the target person in the room beside you, he may wish to ask you questions: "Am I correct in the decision I am about to take?" or "Should I trust my new boss to keep his promise?" To deal with this you will find yourself having to shift back into the Step 2 attitude—the buoyant, elevated demand phase. However, directing your psi to a specific question is not at all an easy task. Psi seems to have its own inclinations! You can *try* to direct it toward a person or thing, but what it will pick up is another matter altogether. For this reason it's best to leave sessions rather freewheeling to begin with, especially until you begin to learn from trial and error what your images mean—your ESP code, as it were. Helpful target persons can aid you here, for as already mentioned they will provide the keys to the correct interpretation of the successful images, and sometimes even those that may not look so successful on the surface.

ESP ETHICS

If you develop a certain amount of proficiency at this technique, friends and friends of friends may at some point start seeking you out for psychic counseling. You could conceivably find yourself turning into the local fortune-teller, which, even if it begins by being flattering, becomes less so after a short while.

Should you allow yourself to become such a psychic sounding board, however, you will sooner or later find yourself confronted by the problem of what to say and what to hold back. For instance, what do you say when you see what seem to you very clear disaster images? If you mention them, decisions will undoubtedly be swayed, consciously or not. Even if the images turn out to have been perfectly accurate, damage can be done simply by telling your subject about them. If you will recall the importance of a person's positive orientation in life, the potential effect of such negative suggestions becomes apparent. All these, I believe, are good reasons for keeping counseling sessions on a game level until you gain skill in handling such situations. At the very least, an "it's-all-a-game" disclaimer allows your sitter to take what you say with a grain of salt should an out be needed. In any case be chary of handing out advice based solely on the evidence of your ESP. It's never, by any means, infallible, even among the most talented sensitives.

OBJECT READING

Object reading, or psychometry, is accomplished like people reading, but at one stage removed. Instead of focusing on the psi field of another person, you theoretically confront a mixture of psi fields clustered about an object.[10] The predominant field may derive from that of any one of its previous owners.

Many professional sensitives, men and women whose psi is

so developed that they are able to use it in helping others, ask for an object belonging to the person on whose behalf they are working, to accentuate the link to their psi field. The psi field of the object in many instances appears to remain joined in some strange way to the psi field of the owner even when he is absent, so a sensitive can sometimes track down the whereabouts of a missing person by concentrating on a piece of clothing or even a photograph of him. Gerard Croiset often works in this manner when he helps the police. So does Olof Jonsson, the remarkable Swedish sensitive who conducted the interplanetary ESP test with Captain Edgar Mitchell aboard Apollo 14.

Psychometrists maintain that the fewer the number of people who have handled an object, the clearer their response to it will be. W. G. Roll in his review of psychometric experiments [11] observed evidence that the psi impressions linked to an object obeyed laws similar to those that govern the mental association of pairs of ideas, with the object itself in this case forming one-half of the pair. Briefly stated, these laws are as follows:

PRIMARY LAWS OF IDEA ASSOCIATION

1. *By contiguity.* Ideas, and thence words, deriving from memories of past experiences tend to become associated by their proximity in time or space. For instance, someone says the word "wasp," and without thinking you answer "picnic." Your idea of a wasp recalls a memory of the picnic where you were once stung by one.

2. *By similarity.* Ideas of a similar nature will often be associated together. Somebody says "wasp" and you respond "needle," because of the painful jab they both can give.

SECONDARY LAWS OF IDEA ASSOCIATION

In the event of a *multiplicity* of associations, these laws decide which will predominate.

1. *Primacy of association.* Ideas will be strongly linked if your

first experience of one happened in association with the other. For instance, someone says "wasp" and you respond "jelly" because the first time you saw one up close was in a jelly jar.

2. *Recency of association.* Recently associated ideas hang together too. The word "wasp" makes you answer "dish towel," because only this morning you flipped a wasp out the window with one.

3. *Frequency of association.* Frequently associated words or ideas tend to stick. E.g., someone says "wasp" and you shoot back "waist."

4. *Vividness of association.* Pairs of ideas emotionally charged by a personal experience stay strongly associated. Someone says "wasp" and you answer "sting."

The key to idea association obviously lies in the memory. In fact, memory experts put these laws of association to very good use when storing prodigious amounts of information in their heads. Likewise, when a sensitive reads an object, he seems to be using it as one-half of a pair of associated ideas; the other half being not his own memory but that of its previous owner. He uses the object to draw out this associated memory.

The type of memory that seems to charge an object in this way most powerfully is one derived from an *emotionally* vivid experience (Secondary Law 4). If one of the previous owners experienced an intense emotion in connection with an object, or even if he had it about him when such an emotion occurred, the object will most likely appear charged with this particular memory when it is psychometrized. An object's *frequency* or *recency* of use also seems to enable sensitives to read it, although not so easily as does vividness of experience, leading one to speculate on whether a psi charge may not fade with time or, conversely, be strengthened by continual use of its carrier object.

OBJECT-READING PROCEDURE

Sensitives receive psi impressions from objects in different ways. Some feel they need to handle the object, while others do not. Try holding, say, a key ring belonging to a stranger and following the same steps as you would for people reading. Instead of concentrating your demand upon a person, focus it upon the key ring. Many sensitives, like Peter Hurkos, find it helps to play with the object continually, to pass it from hand to hand or flutter their fingers on it. The continuous making and breaking of physical contact in some way seems to keep reaffirming the object's reality to the sensitive. Whether the action is just a psychological prop or whether it performs some specific function associated with the psi field, we do not know. Maybe a bit of both.

So when you read an object, try moving it around in your hand, watching the pictures behind your eyelids as usual but also attending to any stray memories or incidents that seem to pop up in your head. Again, resist the temptation to guess or embroider, however fragmentary the imagery at first. If you get nothing, don't strain it. Leave it alone for a while and return to the task later. In the intervening period of time, you may find latency has completed the assignment for you, and you now have a good flow of images. Eileen Garrett says that her psychometric pictures often resemble frozen tableaus: "woodcuts relating to some 'dramatic tangle,'" is the way she expresses it.[12] Words or whole sentences may also come. You may even sense an imaginary taste or odor.

Again, a helpful owner will not only aid you in unraveling your perceptions but also help you in distinguishing the feeling of the correct ones.

SIX

Tracking Down Past Incarnations

Some of the most intriguing psychic research being done today is in the field of reincarnation. Up until recently the very word was a bane to most parapsychologists, associated in their minds with the most crackpot variety of occultism. Now the position looks a little different. Dr. Ian D. Stevenson of the Department of Neurology and Psychiatry at the University of Virginia School of Medicine has been collecting impressive evidence of what, on the surface, look like genuine instances of reincarnation: children who claim to remember memories of past lives that are subsequently verified by the still-living members of their "old" families.[1]

Understandably, the majority of these cases have been collected from communities where reincarnation is believed in —among the Tlingits of Alaska, the Hindus and Buddhists of India, the Druses of Lebanon and the spiritualists of Brazil. Does this mean that a climate of belief or disbelief affects the phenomenon, as it can do with other psi manifestations? Or is it simply that a willingness to believe in it opens the door to a new type of fraud? Inasmuch as the child who claims to be the reborn soul of a deceased member of a wealthy family obviously could stand to gain definite material advantage from being accepted as such, the possibility should at least be considered. Interestingly enough, however, in a number of instances quite the reverse

situation has been noted. Instead of identifying with a pres-
tigious dead person, the child has claimed to remember incidents
in the past life of a social undesirable, such as an executed
murderer.[2]

Such reincarnation memories usually are discouraged by the
parents of the child, who tend to feel intruded upon, quite
understandably experiencing a sense of alienation, a feeling of
having a cuckoo in the nest. Generally, the alien memories seem
to fade as the child grows older and his own personality and
stock of experiences develop. Whether instances of alien
memories like these give evidence for reincarnation or the
equally traditional phenomenon of spirit possession is still
highly uncertain. Possibly the distinction between the two concepts is an academic one. Both are a little more understandable,
perhaps, in the light of the theory of the psi field. An unattached
psi field (unattached by reason of the death of its host body) for
some reason becomes drawn toward the field of a young child,
producing symptoms of personality "leakage" and the appearance of alien memories in the same way that the psi field of a
target object does to the field of a psychometrist.

Is it possible, then, that all of us perhaps harbor "orphan" psi
fields of this type, perhaps accessible only in the deeper stages of
trance? Could such a theory help to explain such extraordinary
occurrences of secondary personality as "Patience Worth," the
alter ego of Mrs. John Curran, an uneducated middle-class
housewife from St. Louis? Not only did "Patience Worth" claim
to have lived in Dorset, England, in the sixteenth century, but she
also proceeded to write reams of poetry in the vernacular of that
day, as well as a series of historically accurate novels that seemed
far beyond the inventive skill and intellectual grasp of Mrs.
Curran.[3]

TECHNIQUES FOR REMEMBERING "PAST LIVES"

Unlike most Hindus and Buddhists, who seem to feel that
past lives should remain things of the past, adherents of the cult

of Theosophy, which originated in the nineteenth century and loosely bases its tenets on those of Hinduism and Buddhism, believe that a knowledge of past lives can often bring benefit and understanding to one's present existence. They have accordingly evolved mental exercises to aid in the recovery of these hypothetical memories. Whether these exercises just dredge up free-floating ESP impressions, one's own unconscious fantasies or real glimpses of past incarnations, as Theosophists claim, is of course impossible to say. If you're intrigued by the idea of reincarnation, whatever the explanation of evidence in its favor turns out to be, you may care to try the exercises for yourself. Whereas Mrs. Curran used automatic writing, these use dreaming—our chief natural fishing line to the unconscious mind.

1. Before going to sleep each night, write down your intention to fish for memories of your past incarnations. Then, as you drift off, mentally review the activities of the day *backward*, beginning where you are now and ending with your awakening the previous morning. You will probably find this difficult to do at first, and may only be able to jump from remembered incident to remembered incident, leaving out the bulk of the day's activities to begin with. Keep at it for a few evenings, and soon you will find yourself able to unreel the chief memories of your day as if you were unreeling a roll of film. Actually, it doesn't matter if you skip a few incidents or even if you don't finish the exercise before you fall asleep—it's the reversing of "direction" that counts. Obviously we are not actually penetrating the past in this way: A more likely rationale would lie in the area of suggestibility. By running our memories backward, maybe we are simply giving our minds a neatly enacted *suggestion* of reaching back into the past.

2. As you fall asleep, try to keep one last spark of attention aware of the dream images that begin to unfold before you. Psychologists refer to these visions as hypnogogic dreams: dreams that lead to sleep. You will note they have a strongly electric and alive quality sometimes, quite unlike one's usual remembered dreams. This may be due to the fact that one is still

semiconscious while one experiences them, and they may well be related if not identical to lucid dreams. Like any other type of dream, hypnogogic dreams can and do become channels for ESP scanning. For "reincarnation" exploration, however, you should keep your mental eyes open for dream images of houses, rooms, voices, faces, even songs that you feel you recognize. The telltale sign of a genuine reincarnation memory is said to be the sudden, overwhelming rush of nostalgia it brings.

3. If you do obtain one of these possible memory fragments, jot down notes about it on a pad beside your bed so it isn't forgotten by the morning. Then return to it as you drift off again, using it as a thread to pull out other associated memories, as a psychometrist does with his target object.

4. Once you obtain what you feel might be genuine memories, you can abandon your unraveling exercises. Their purpose has been accomplished, and your "memory" now becomes the center of your attention.

Try various of your other ESP techniques on it: For instance, while holding one "memory" in mind, try your ESP-vision technique and see if any interesting or apparently relevant images appear. If they do, again make notes about them first before pursuing them. (The reason, of course, for this note taking is to *fix* any perceptions we obtain. ESP impressions of any sort are frequently fleeting and usually vanish without trace unless they are remarkable enough to trigger a very strong reaction in you.)

You can also now try for names and dates, using a pendulum or, better still, the glass game or Ouija board with a group of your friends. Also note any real dreams you have that seem to have a bearing on the subject.

About the farthest I've ever managed to progress with this technique is to get nostalgic feelings that I associate with a recurring dream I've had since my childhood concerning Richmond Hill, a part of London I have never lived in. If I do have a recollection of dates and names, they remain stubbornly buried. Maybe just as well!

If you are lucky enough to come up with something as

concrete as a familiar-sounding name or place, then you can of course begin tracking it down from an objective standpoint as well. However, the world is a very large place to search, especially when we also have to consider the added dimension of time. Searches of this sort obviously are the needle-in-the-haystack variety unless we can come up with a historical marker or a specific occurrence, perhaps recorded in local newspapers. Newspaper files, church registers and old telephone directories are three very useful sources of information. Street and other detailed maps can also be very helpful. If you have the time, nothing, of course, can beat paying a suspected location a visit.

It does occasionally happen that alien "memories" are touched off when a person visits some faraway place on a vacation and starts "remembering" it as it used to be. Coincidence? Simple ESP? Retrocognition? Reincarnation? Who knows? Even ruling out coincidence, it's very difficult to decide among the other three. Whatever the explanation, it remains an intriguing phenomenon and one that has received less attention than it possibly deserves. Even if one cannot come up with a satisfactory explanation for a "memory" of this sort, it gives one plenty of food for thought, and maybe even helps one to confront the scary idea of death with a little more equanimity.

SEVEN

The Out-of-the-Body Experience

One of the most mysterious and possibly most significant of all psychic experiences is so-called traveling clairvoyance or astral projection, today referred to by parapsychologists as the out-of-the-body experience. In psi literature this phrase is usually shortened to the initials OOBE or OBE.[1]

Unlike in a lucid dream, where the dreamer, although achieving self-awareness, continues to participate in the imaginary events conjured up by his own mind, the person who experiences astral projection finds himself situated among his everyday physical surroundings in an apparently disembodied state. A common astral projection experience, and generally a rather alarming one, is seeing one's own inert physical body from this out-of-the-body vantage point. Cases of involuntary OBE have been reported by people involved in near-fatal accidents or illness, as well as by mediums and sensitives who are sometimes able to turn the OBE on and off at will.[2] Parapsychologists, though acknowledging the occurrence of the phenomenon, are still very much in the dark about its nature, let alone its explanation. Is it simply an hallucination, perhaps fed by genuinely psi-mediated information, or is something really projected out of one's physical body? Maybe OBE represents a complete switch of awareness from the sense organs of the body to the entire psi field, a return to the primitive global method of sensing? Most importantly, does this something survive death? [3] If the current research into the possibilities of reincarnation provides any solace for the thought of death, then OBE research may turn out to do the job even more effectively, although we haven't arrived at any comfortably reassuring evidential plateaus yet.

As far back as the 1880's Frederic Myers and Edmund Gurney, two of the founders of the SPR, speculated that the out-of-the-body phenomenon might provide the key to the entire range of our psychic powers, since it apparently indicates an ability possessed by some people to exist and function outside the confines of their physical bodies. Myers collaborated with Gurney and Frank Podmore, curiously enough a staunch disbeliever in postmortem survival, in compiling what amounted to an encyclopedia of reports concerning the visitation of living people by the apparent ghosts of other *living* people.[4] Such "phantasms of the living" can be experienced reciprocally, moreover: The person whose "ghost" is perceived can feel he or she is actually in the presence of the person to whom it is at the time appearing.

Gurney explained such occurrences as mutually experienced telepathic hallucinations, although many psychic researchers have continued to favor the idea of an externalized astral double: a body composed of some type of mysterious psychic energy that does the actual traveling and communicating. At first sight the astral-body theory looks a reasonable one, tying in nicely with old notions about ghosts and spirits. However, Myers and Gurney's hallucination theory fits the bill even better, if by hallucination we understand not a haphazard mental delusion but rather the activation of those brain processes that give us our senses of seeing, smelling, feeling, tasting and hearing. In cases of astral projection the activation would be triggered by some unseen psi signal rather than a physical object in the vicinity. Such a theory would also fit well into the concept of mutually interacting psi fields within a psi continuum, and it also does away with the necessity of theorizing in unwieldy nine-teenth-century mechanical terms about phantom ectoplasmic limbs and so on.

Maybe the following analogy can help to clarify the idea a little: Imagine a highly developed two-way television circuit that not only provides a three-dimensional picture of its target but also stimulates the other senses of touch, taste, hearing and smell. Such a system would provide a highly convincing experience of the target, and you would find it extremely difficult to tell the illusion from the reality. Now let's take the analogy one stage further: If the TV circuit were in some way part of your biological equipment, something you were born with, you might begin to consider yourself justified in your view that what you were experiencing *was* reality, that you were really in the actual presence of what you were viewing and touching and hearing. That you knew, intellectually, you were separated from the target by several miles would be almost beside the point. The translation of electronic impulses into your sense experience would of course be taking place where your physical body was, but your *experience itself* would seem to you to be occurring in the target's vicinity.

If the out-of-the-body experience does represent a translation of psi-field data into a sensory hallucination, it raises a further question. In spontaneous cases of OBE occurring during accidents or grave illness, the experiencer frequently shows all medically recognized signs of being unconscious. So where in his body is the experience being registered? Certainly not in what is today considered to be the thinking part of his brain. Is it possible that we can in some way think and experience things with our sympathetic or parasympathetic nervous systems *as well as* with our brains? Or does something really exist alongside or in coincidence with my physical body, something that is capable of thought and experience, something that is "me" as much as my body is? Furthermore, can this something function independently of my body and perhaps even survive death?

OBE RESEARCH TODAY

Postmortem-survival research is today being conducted by three parapsychological organizations: the American Society for Psychical Research, the Parapsychology Division of the University of Virginia and the Psychical Research Foundation. All are concentrating their attention on living subjects who have a history of OBE's. The reason they are taking this approach instead of simply arranging séances with mediums is a practical one: Nobody, least of all a parapsychologist, knows whether a medium's "spirit communications" really come from the souls of the departed or are a result of the medium's own psi powers finding things out and dramatizing them. So we don't have bona fide spirits of the dead on hand to experiment with—at least none that could not be explained away as something else. But we do have those of the living—our own (going on the assumption for the sake of argument that such things as spirits exist).

This brings us to the crux of the matter: We must see if we can detect any objective evidence of someone's spirit, soul, psi field or whatever else we wish to call it that is capable of functioning outside the recognized confines of the body. The place to begin such a search would surely be with those people who claim to have experienced just such a disembodied state of consciousness. Once we have established this experience as a detectable laboratory fact we can start performing experiments with it. Only after we have assembled enough data from these experiments can we start speculating with any degree of assurance about whether this state of awareness points to the existence of what we can call a soul or spirit that "lives on" after death.

I put "lives on" in quotes, for again, the question becomes a philosophical one when we pause to consider it for a moment. "Lives on" assumes time and space to do the living in. Our experience of time and space is entirely conditioned by our physical bodies. Our bodies, in effect, *produce* time and space for us by their size and their comparative rates of metabolic change. Without going into a major philosophical digression, assuming for the sake of argument that the OBE represents an expansion of our psi-field awareness and a tuning-out of the physical body and its conditions, is there any real reason why such an awareness or even spirit existence should retain any of our body-conditioned concepts of time and space? At that point of awareness or being, such concepts may indeed become empty of any kind of meaning.

Both the ASPR and PRF researchers are applying strict laboratory controls to their OBE subjects, measuring their heart rates, brain waves and respiration rates. They also check them for dream activity by watching for telltale rapid eye movements—side-to-side movements that scientists now know our eyes make when we're dreaming, as if we were watching a drama unfold on a wide-angle movie screen.

Definite tasks are set for the OBE subjects, such as to observe hidden targets while in the OBE state. Targets are sometimes reflected in mirrors to see if their OBE vision obeys the same laws of optics as everyday vision.[5] The target areas to which the astral projections are being directed are monitored for any changes in their electromagnetic fields, temperature, light levels and so on.

OUT-OF-THE-BODY TECHNIQUES

The first OBE experimenters relied chiefly on hypnotism to induce out-of-the-body states in their subjects. In those days they believed that hypnosis was caused by the radiation of mysterious beams of "animal magnetism" emanating from the hypnotist, an idea that we shall be returning to later when we take a look at psychokinesis.

Lieutenant Colonel Eugène de Rochas, a one-time administrator of the Ecole Polytechnique of Paris, conducted a series of experiments with a blindfolded, hypnotized subject at the turn of the century and discovered that she was able to feel pinpricks made in the air several inches from her body.[6] De Rochas advanced the theory that this apparent exteriorization of her sensitivity was due to the presence of her partially dislodged spirit double. Hippolyte Baraduc, a contemporary of de Rochas, proposed that these emanations were the same as the much-vaunted animal magnetism of the day and were simply rays of nerve force radiating from the body.

Hector Durville, another French researcher, followed up de Rochas and Baraduc's hypnotic experiments with his own, using as a theoretical framework the by then famous work of Gurney, Myers and Podmore, even to the extent of appropriating their title, *Phantasms of the Living*, for his own book, *Le Fantôme des Vivants*.[7] He and another investigator in the field, Charles Lancelin,[8] became in large measure responsible for the notion that astral projection could be voluntarily induced.

It was, however, a spiritualist medium, Minnie E. Keeler, who provided the lore of astral projection with its chief techniques. Mrs. Keeler claimed these techniques, which really amounted more to fragmentary suggestions than to exercises, were dictated to her by spirit communicators in the time-honored way. Mrs. Keeler's astral-projection techniques were noted by Prescott F. Hall, a skeptical contributor to the *Journal of the American Society for Psychical Research*, who included them in the 1916 edition of the *Journal*.[9] A couple of years later he followed these articles up with an account of the investigations of the techniques he had himself conducted.[10] His interest in the techniques was a mixed one, however, for he was initially more concerned with proving or disproving the reality of Mrs. Keeler's alleged communicators. He reasoned that if they really existed outside Mrs. Keeler's imagination, they might well corroborate this fact by providing workable astral-projection techniques unknown to occultism or psychic research.

The partial successes Hall obtained by using these exercises prompted Hereward Carrington, a well-known author of books on psychic research and an officer of both the English and American Societies for Psychical Research, to include them in one of his books.[11] One of his readers, Sylvan J. Muldoon, subsequently wrote him that since his childhood he had experienced out-of-the-body states similar to those described by Carrington. Muldoon and Carrington's follow-up book, *The Projection of the Astral Body*,[12] fleshed out Mrs. Keeler's astral-projection exercises and supplemented them with those of Oliver Fox, another spontaneous experient who had published details of his experiments a few years previously, in 1920.[13]

Since the publication of Muldoon and Carrington's book, a considerable number of other OBE methods have been evolved, most of them derivative from Fox and Keeler wholly or in part. One recent exception to the rule is the method described by OBE experient Robert A. Monroe.[14] We shall be taking a look at his and the various other techniques shortly.

Aside from a couple of precautions, the techniques themselves are simple enough, like all psi exercises, but their proponents claim they need to be persevered in unless you have a natural aptitude. As in all psi experiments, our first and perhaps most important consideration, according to OBE experts, is our attitude. We must really want to achieve an out-of-the-body experience and be willing to direct our attention wholeheartedly to that end. In terms of our rationale, these, like all psychic techniques, are simply means to an end. Meditation, hypnosis, repetition, knot-tying, whatever the device, in the last analysis it always seems to boil down to a game we play with our mind to direct its attention and at the same time trick it into a psychologically unblocked condition that will allow us access to our psi fields.

DIET

Mrs. Keeler, perhaps in accordance with the occult fads of the turn of the century, advised the would-be astral traveler to abstain from meat and adhere to a vegetarian diet. Fruit, especially prunes, was considered to be good for astral projection. Raw eggs would supply the projector with his proteins. Carrots were beneficial, but nuts were not. Peanuts were considered particularly bad for some reason. Drugs, alcohol and tobacco were, of course, out of the question. Fasting in general was said to be good. Mrs. Keeler also added (perhaps for the benefit of those who were already quailing at the thought of such a Spartan existence) that once proficiency in the projection techniques was obtained in five to six months, the dietary rules could cheerfully be abandoned.[15]

Bogus as these strictures may sound, there may well be a grain of sense to them. Setting aside the known values of fresh fruit and vegetables and the dulling effects of drugs, fasting itself when maintained over long periods of time can not only sharpen one's mind but also dispose one to hallucination (or astral projection, depending on one's point of view). It's also well known that sleeping on an empty stomach as well as on an overfull one can cause one to dream excessively. Muldoon actually recommended going to sleep hungry or thirsty, sometimes placing a glass of water strategically in another room of the house as bait to lure your astral body out of its physical counterpart.[16] (Of course, under such circumstances one could equally well be said to have experienced a wish-fulfillment dream about the water rather than an astral projection.) So even if the vegetarian diet recommended by Mrs. Keeler had in itself no effect on the phenomenon, the reduction of one's food intake might well do so.[17]

TIME FACTORS

Most OBE experients find that the time of the attempt is not important, although those with an occult bent maintain that they function best, astrally speaking, during the full moon. Charles Lancelin recommended the period between 11:00 P.M. and 3:00 A.M.; that is, when one usually is sleeping. He also added, perhaps because of suspicions he had about the phenomenon's being in some way related to electricity, that it is best attempted during dry, clear weather, with a high barometer, no thunderstorm about and an air temperature in the 70's.[18]

POSITION OF THE BODY

Mrs. Keeler recommended sitting erect, hands and feet uncrossed, with eyes closed, in a darkened room. Muldoon, however, maintained that lying on his back was the most conducive position for him. It also happens to be one of the positions most conducive to dreaming—I very rarely sleep on my back, because when I do I almost invariably dream excessively or experience nightmares.

Monroe recommends lying on one's side on a north-south axis, with one's head to the north. He also advocates that no tight clothing be worn (as does Mrs. Keeler) and, interestingly, no metals, which, along with the geomagnetic orientation again points to his underlying belief in some electromagnetic aspect of the phenomenon.[19]

BREATHING EXERCISES

According to both Mrs. Keeler and Muldoon, slowed breathing is an inducement to astral projection. Mrs. Keeler advocated slowing the breathing down by holding the breath *in* (not out).[20] Muldoon carried this suggestion one step further and proposed a progressive relaxation exercise [21] whereby one's attention is to be centered on the slowed-down heartbeat felt in the body, hands, arms, legs and so on. On examination this method seems to be Muldoon's adaptation of psychologist T. H. Schultz's Autogenic Training, a technique of self-hypnosis developed during the mid-1920's whereby the subject progressively attains control by relaxation and suggestion over his circulatory system, heart, respiration and finally head.

For people in normal health this type of experimenting with one's heartbeat probably holds no more physical danger than a strenuous sport. But for those with cardiac problems, I'm sure I hardly need add that it may not be a good idea.

Monroe's approach to breathing appears to be as novel as the rest of his method, for he advocates breathing through a half-closed mouth to develop "vibrations," about which more later.

THE VISUAL FIELD

Both Muldoon and Monroe recommend turning the closed eyes upward and staring into the darkness of one's fore-head—our old vision technique.

MENTAL EXERCISES

Most of the images Mrs. Keeler and Muldoon proposed for visualization seem to derive from occult ideas fashionable in their time. Those of Monroe, on the other hand, seem more characteristic of his technical background—he was at one time involved in the field of cable TV and electronics. We know comparatively little about what goes on in our minds when we practice meditation, and these mental visualizations are no exception to the rule. They may be merely autosuggestive, effective only in their ability to induce a state of dissociation in us; a state of consciousness we mildly experience every time we immerse ourselves in a good book or movie, only to emerge in a slight daze that may last for some time afterward, depending on how involved we become.

In pronounced states of mental dissociation we can shift the focus of our attention far from the structured and safe everyday world of common sense to a teeming, unstructured inner world of unconsciously produced fantasies where anything can happen. Our vision technique may well be a peephole into that world. If you take LSD or mescaline you can find yourself totally immersed in it. Uncontrolled and chronic eruptions of this state of consciousness characterize the mental world of the schizophrenic, and astral projection may well turn out to be part and parcel of the same phenomenon.

It is at this point that the second word of caution should be given. Visualization exercises should never be pushed to the point of hallucination without some sort of objective control in the form of medical or psychiatric supervision being exercised. For most of us, I imagine, this caution is superfluous as we simply don't have the time to pursue exercises of this sort to that length. Altered states of consciousness like these are only reached after months of the sort of repeated practice encountered in a Buddhist monastery or the like. Used in moderation I don't suppose these exercises would harm the average experimenter—at any rate, they haven't harmed me. But they could be pushed to extremes, and this should be avoided. Psychologists Gardner Murphy and Alice E. Moriarty of the Menninger Foundation brought out the distinction between the two degrees of dissociation in their 1967 article, "Some Thoughts about Prerequisite Conditions or States in Creativity and the Paranormal Experience": "By this [psi-useful dissociation], we mean an ability to tolerate the unreal or fanciful; to muse freely without anxiety about lack of definiteness; to become absorbed in ideas, fantasies, or feelings [as differentiated from] the unreality of the schizoid with loss of integration." [22]

Several of the OBE visualizations mentioned by Mrs. Keeler have what we would today call a psychedelic hue. Where she obtained them is anybody's guess. Maybe they were communicated by genuine spirit entities, or by dissociated fragments of her own personality, however you wish to explain the phenomenon of mediumship. Contrary to Prescott Hall's assertion, however, none of them was really very original. Two at least were stock-in-trade meditation exercises of occult groups flourishing around the turn of the century.

VISUALIZATION EXERCISES

(Exercises 1 and 2 are presumably to be performed seated. The position of the physical body is usually supposed to conform to the astral visualization.)

1. Imagine a mirror image of yourself twenty feet behind you. Imagine yourself moving backward toward it.

2. Imagine a mirror image of yourself six feet in front of you. "Urge" yourself toward it.

3. Try to urge yourself eighteen inches above your physical head. (This meditation obviously can be performed seated or lying down. The astral-projection position advocated by Muldoon is lying flat on one's back.)

4. Imagine your astral power steaming out of the pores of your body and condensing into a double above you. (This rather difficult visualization is curiously like a description of the Romanian folklore belief concerning the way in which vampires materialize. The Victorian novelist Bram Stoker has Dracula (1897) appear in the form of such a mist, a condensation of shimmering phosphorescent specks in the air.)

5. Imagine yourself climbing a rope or ladder. (Again, significant from a folklore point of view: Tree, rope or ladder climbing is the ritual by which shamans frequently induce their "spirit-wandering" trances—states of consciousness that by all accounts parallel almost exactly modern reports of out-of-the-body states.[23])

6. Imagine yourself as a point of light floating on top of water in a rapidly filling tank. Your task is to exit through a tiny hole in the roof of the tank. (The "flight through the hole in the roof of the world" is again a recurrent motif in shamanic lore.[24])

7. Imagine what it feels like to breathe through your ears. (Weird as it sounds, this exercise has a definite and very strange effect, as you may notice for yourself if you try it.)

8. Sit erect, with closed eyes, and imagine a horizontal bar above your line of sight. Urge yourself up to see over it (like a chin-up?). Hold your breath in when you get a sensation of rising.

9. Tighten the muscles in your hands and feet and contract your stomach muscles and imagine yourself falling. (This exercise can be performed seated or lying down.)

10. Imagine yourself revolving on tiptoe and then springing off at a tangent. (Seems to be an action somewhere between a balletic *fouetté* and putting the shot!)

11. Imagine a whirlpool. Feel yourself being sucked down through the vortex. Try for a sensation of contraction, then expansion. (The spinning disk with converging spirals is a common hypnotist's prop.)

12. Imagine a twirling star hanging in space. (Mrs. Keeler's communicators proposed this image for the development of astral hearing.)

13. Visualize a spinning disk, and then distend its center so that it grows into a three-dimensional rotating cone or vortex, like a waterspout. Now resolve it back into a disk again. Feel yourself entering the vortex.

14. Imagine yourself carried along on the crest of a wave. (Surfing would obviously be a good memory to draw on here.)

15. Imagine a point of light two feet in front of your throat. Feel it slowly approach. When it reaches you, imagine yourself blending with it and becoming that point of light. (This exercise has obvious affinity with yogic exercises designed to achieve one-pointedness. In Hindu terminology the visualized point of light is known as a seed, *bindu*, with which the yogi is counseled to merge his consciousness.)

16. Seat yourself in a comfortable chair four feet away from a mirror. Staring at your mirror image, repeat your name over and over until it becomes a series of meaningless sounds. Now pretend the person in the mirror is the "real" you.

(This exercise, suggested originally by Mrs. Keeler but elaborated by Muldoon, is a fairly apparent path to self-hypnosis. The feeling of the dual identity striven for is one of the more commonly reported observations of the out-of-body state. A variant of this exercise was evolved by a relative newcomer to the field of OBE, Edward C. Peach, who writes under the name of Ophiel. Before attempting the experiment he recommends [25] that the would-be astral projector spend some time walking around his own home in a prearranged projection route. He should pay particular attention to eight selected spots about the house, memorizing the views he obtains from them. Two of these places should be vantage points looking into the bedroom or wherever else he plans to leave his "empty" physical body during the experiment. When attempting the projection, he must retrace his memorized route in his imagination, endeavoring to "see" these views through his astral eyes. Peach also cleverly suggests associating each of these visual memories with a different, arbitrarily chosen scent like rosewater or ammonia, and also a musical tone. These olfactory and auditory memories help to add dimension to the visual ones, assisting in recall when he tries to summon them up in his imagination.[26])

17. Robert Monroe's technique clearly deserves a paragraph to itself because of its explicitness and originality. While similar in essence to the Keeler-Muldoon techniques, Munroe's relies on technological analogies rather than occult ones. According to him, the OBE experient must lie down on his side, his head to the north, his mouth half open, staring with closed eyes into the darkness of his forehead. He must now try to direct his gaze one foot ahead into the darkness; that is, allow his eyes to converge as if he were genuinely focusing on something one foot away. This distance must then be lengthened to around three feet, and then angled straight up in the air until one's eyes are looking up at a 30-degree angle to the horizontal. Once this inner-space coordinate has been approximated, Monroe counsels the OBE projector to "reach" for this position, to zero in upon it in a way that suggests Mrs. Keeler's instructions to urge oneself up or away from the physical body.

At this time, Monroe asserts, one may experience a curious rumbling, hissing, pulsating sensation that will surge from head to toe and back again. Monroe's description of this pulsation makes it sound very like the surge of current in a radio circuit. He even managed to ascertain the frequency of his own pulsations at around 27 cycles per second. Acknowledging that they may in some way be connected with his open-mouthed breathing, Monroe advocates that these mysterious pulsations be speeded up until they form a continuous vibration, analogous to a smoothly running motor. After this point, Monroe warns the experimenter, there is no turning back. He will have cut loose from the ties of earth and must now be prepared for unexpected (and not necessarily pleasant) excursions into the astral world. These, judging by the descriptions he gives of his fantastic experiences, sound more like visions or lucid dreams than OBE's in the generally accepted sense of the word.[27]

18. Oliver Fox was a student in a technical college during the 1920's when he experienced and wrote about his experiences of astral projection. Muldoon and Carrington included Fox's "dream-control" method of projection in their book, and Muldoon himself elaborated upon it. Fox advises the researcher to practice dream recall until he reaches a point where he begins to experience lucid dreams. At this point—which is usually marked physiologically by the acceleration of brain activity—the experimenter will tend to awaken. However, if he makes an effort to hold himself in the borderline condition between waking and dreaming, Fox maintains that with practice this can lead to an experience of astral projection. By holding this in-between state of consciousness Fox found he could pre-cipitate what he described as a mental "click," followed by a reawakening in the astral body that was often characterized by an awareness of his own inert body lying on the bed as seen from several feet away.

Muldoon's variant of this method was to invent a dream scenario for himself—a little fantasy involving movement of some variety: swimming, flying, ballooning or an elevator ride—which he would then slip into just before he fell asleep at night. The movement itself had to reflect the position in which he was lying in bed—e.g., in the elevator ride he had to imagine he was lying on his back on the car's floor. According to Muldoon, the repeated use of this technique facilitated his nightly astral excursions.

OBE STATES

Experiences of the astral world tend to differ from account to account. The one consistently recurring observation seems to be that the lighting, often of a bluish-gray cast, tends to be indirect, suffusing everything. The dreamlike and in some instances contradictory descriptions appear to point to a dream basis for the phenomenon, although details of distant events reported after such astral projections and subsequently verified also suggest some type of psi involvement. Whether there are degrees of purity of OBE consciousness—that is, states in which one is completely and objectively aware of external reality, as contrasted to states in which one is primarily involved in the productions of one's own unconscious mind (lucid dreaming)—remains to be investigated. It is possible that OBE's extend along a spectrum of which the two extremities are subjective and objective. Interestingly enough, Mrs. Keeler counsels against having any expectations about what one will see on the astral plane, stating as a reason that any such expectations will only tend to produce illusions generated by one's own mind; an indication that she (or her communicators) partially understood the subjective quality of the experience.

OBE LOCOMOTION

According to all OBE experients, movement in the OBE state is accomplished by simply thinking hard of where one wishes to go. Fox advocates horizontal gliding or flying as the best means of astral travel. Monroe describes the process as "thinking light" and formulating the desire to "lift off." He also recounts a method of "rotating" astrally off one's bed, like a log turning over in the water. If you've ever rolled off an air mattress in a swimming pool, you'll probably have a good idea of this technique. Indeed, it strikes me that many of the sensations described by astral projectors may well derive from early memories of swimming: that first ecstatic time one took one's feet off the ground and floated independently.

Monroe also advocates thinking of a person rather than a place to visit, rotating until you "feel" you are pointing in the right direction and then holding your hands above your head and stretching, reaching toward the goal. Memories of diving lessons, perhaps, or even shades of Superman? If this phenomenon does pertain to the category of lucid dreaming, then obviously the memory images must come from somewhere, and I suspect childhood is the best place to look for them.

Return to the physical body usually happens all too easily, according to most accounts. If a return is required, a simple desire to wake up or just a thought about one's physical body is usually sufficient to bring one back. Many experients maintain that on returning to physical consciousness they feel, rather alarmingly, a few moments of physical paralysis. Monroe advises one to swallow, move the tongue and generally concentrate on moving the limbs until normal feeling is restored.

SUMMING UP

By all accounts, then, there seem to be basically two ways by which we can voluntarily enter the OBE state: through the repeated cultivation of our "dream ego" in lucid dreams, which, according to various accounts, can and will lapse over into an OBE; and by cultivating various states of mental dissociation, of which the most extreme are probably best experimented with under some sort of medical supervision. The fact that involuntary OBE's often seem to occur as a result of violent physical trauma or shock should speak for itself.

To reiterate, we do not yet understand the true nature of the experience these exercises produce—whether they are interesting hallucinations, global psi awareness, vivid dreams or bona fide traveling in a secondary spirit body—but we do know that the phenomenon exists and that one day it will have to be explained. If you know or discover you have an OBE aptitude and feel so inclined, write to the ASPR or PRF about it.[28] Should your experience be of sufficient interest and in accord with their current line of investigation, they may well ask you to participate in one of their research programs.

EIGHT

Psychokinesis—Mind over Matter?

The belief that one can control the fall of dice by willpower is not unusual among professional crapshooters. In 1934 Dr. Rhine received a visit in his Duke University office from just such a gambler. He had come, he announced, to draw Rhine's attention to this curious talent he believed he possessed.

The young man's claim, and the experiments Rhine conducted as a result of it, opened up the fourth and, to the physicist, the most interesting area of psi activity studied today: psychokinesis (PK), the power the mind seems to possess of influencing matter.

Dr. Rhine's psychokinesis tests followed the line of thought suggested by his visitor. They involved mechanically thrown dice that the subject wills to fall with a certain face uppermost. Statistics collected over the years by Rhine and others indicate that higher-than-chance scores can indeed be obtained in this way.[1]

Rhine proposed that PK was the other side of the coin from ESP: output psi rather than input psi. Many parapsychologists today use this suggestion as a working hypothesis. The fact that strong PK producers have often been seen to demonstrate significant scores in ESP tests would seem to support the theory.

Such a theory, however, only goes part of the way in explaining the riddle of PK. The question arises: Where does the energy to do the work of dice tipping come from? You can't get something for nothing—there's always a price tag in physics. The small amount of electricity given off by the agent's brain and nervous system seems inadequate for the task although conceivably it might act as a trigger for a force of some other type.

Haakon Forwald, a Swedish engineer and inventor of considerable skill, introduced a variant of Rhine's PK test, the Placement Test, to see if he could pin down the source of this mysterious energy. In Placement Tests, the subject tries to will a falling die into a selected area of the board rather than simply concentrate on making a specified face fall uppermost. Forwald theorized at first that the energy needed to make dice fall in the desired positions might be drawn from their atomic structures. Try as he might to record significant atomic activity, however, his tests all drew blanks, leaving parapsychology with yet one more negative item of information: PK is not some strange sort of radioactivity.[2]

Another curious fact that emerged from both Rhine's and Forwald's tests is that the number of dice used in the experiment does not seem to affect the outcome. Nor does their size or weight, which leads one to suspect that some type of blanket field of force like gravity is involved, something that can deal as easily with two dice as it can with ten. Either that or, as PK skeptics maintain, PK force is simply a quirk of statistics.

HELMUT SCHMIDT'S EXPERIMENTS

This particular objection was settled once and for all in the late 1960's when a further and historically most important nugget of PK information was dug up by Dr. Helmut Schmidt, a research physicist from the Plasma Physics Laboratory at Boeing in Seattle. Dr. Schmidt's experiments indicated that PK operates not only on a grand scale with dice but also on a microphysical one with atomic particles. Schmidt found his subjects were apparently able to influence mentally the supposedly random choice of an electronic two-number generator. The machine's choice of one of its two numbers depended on a high-frequency switch oscillating between two positions. The switch would stop at one of these positions only when caused to do so by the emission of a beta particle, an electron given out by the nucleus of a nearby radioactive isotope—theoretically one of the most random and undeterminable events in nature.[3] From their positive scoring, it appeared that Schmidt's subjects were psychokinetically tinkering either with the rate of radioactive decay of the strontium 90 isotope or with the switch mechanism itself.

Schmidt elaborated upon his original experiment in 1973. Instead of using a simple number generator, he worked with a complex one that based its final choice of number on a "majority vote count" of a rapid sequence of one hundred random events, this time produced by the amplitude of randomly generated electronic noise rather than radioactive decay. Again Schmidt attained positive results,[4] which seems to rule out the second option: psychokinetic tampering with the switch mechanism. Needless to say, Schmidt also ran identical control tests with his number generators without any attempted mental influence, and, as one would expect, the results showed simple chance levels of significance.

Judging by the lively interest Schmidt's experiments have stirred up in the international scientific community, they may well mark a turning point in the course of experimental psychic research. For the first time in the history of science, hard, *mechanical* evidence of the mind's ability to interfere with distant events has been produced, something very difficult to pooh-pooh away as mere statistical juggling. Now all we need is a workable theory to account for the results!

If PK energy is drawn from the objects affected, all the sensitive instruments used so far have failed to detect it. Again the same old psi problem is rearing its head, this time wearing a PK hat rather than an ESP one: We see the effect, but where is its connection with its cause? Jung's theory of synchronicity really seems to be a fancy way of begging the question, although maybe he was working along the right lines. Could the cause, one wonders, be something so fundamental, like the water surrounding a fish or the air we breathe, that we normally take it for granted because of its obviousness? What on earth could that be?

Before even attempting to approach this problem, which has baffled the best brains in the field, we should first take a look at what today is believed to be another highly important aspect of PK: poltergeist phenomena. They may well shed some light on the situation.

ARE POLTERGEISTS UNCONSCIOUS PK?

Mysterious movements and inexplicable breakages of objects have been recorded since way back in history. They frequently seem to happen in the vicinity of one person who, because of the sometimes mischievous quality of the occurrences, used to be considered to have been singled out for persecution by a ghost or demon referred to as a "poltergeist," a German word meaning "noisy spirit."

The so-called Demon Drummer of Tedworth, a poltergeist that invaded the house of a seventeenth-century English magistrate for two years, is a case in point. The phenomenon was fully documented in Joseph Glanvill's book about witchcraft and inexplicable events, *Sadducismus Triumphatus*, described in the author's words as a "small collection of the most credible and best attested stories." Obviously we should normally take the story with more than a grain of salt, save for the details, which do happen to conform to the classic poltergeist pattern. Objects moved about, phantom lights were seen and deafening thumping and drumming sounds were heard that frequently wakened the entire village of Tedworth. The phenomena were thought to have been triggered by the curse of a vagrant drummer who had had his drum confiscated by the magistrate. Only when the unlucky drummer was physically deported from the country did the disturbances cease, although they resumed with renewed vigor when he managed to make his way back to England again.

One of the more dangerous and unpleasant tricks attributed to the poltergeist is that of stone-throwing. Probably the earliest record we have of this type of stunt dates back to the year 858 when stones thrown by, it was believed, a malignant demon rained down upon the walls of the houses of Bingen on the Rhine.

In many cases poltergeist-thrown stones, when observed in flight, appear to move in slow motion, sometimes parallel to the ground. Occasionally they have been observed to drop from the ceilings of rooms, materializing mysteriously en route. Not only stone falls of this sort have been recorded, but equally alarming falls of liquid, too. In 1905 in the little Calabrian village of Tessano one unlucky old woman, after first experiencing the terrors of a barrage of poltergeist-thrown objects, was subjected to the ludicrous phenomenon of just such an interior deluge: "a great quantity of water" that "began to fall from the ceiling onto her bed and even on her person, following her about all over the house," according to the local press report.[5]

Outbreaks of poltergeist activity, far from being confined to the superstitious past, still happen today. In one dramatic and well-documented (even videotaped) case that occurred recently in a law office at Rosenheim, a small Bavarian town near the Austrian border, lightbulbs exploded, fuses blew and phantom telephone calls were registered, apparently indicating mysterious surges of electrical current in the office wiring. The Rosenheim Maintenance Department was summoned to investigate and found that some of the fuses were supporting a current of up to 50 amperes, way over their limit, and, equally mysteriously, were somehow remaining intact. The phone company was called in and by means of a counter ascertained that the phantom calls were attributable to the time number being dialed up to four or five times a minute, sometimes forty or fifty times in succession.

At this point, normal(!) poltergeist activity began to occur: Pictures rotated on the walls, file drawers opened by themselves and ceiling lamps inexplicably swayed. Three experts were called in to investigate: parapsychologist Dr. Hans Bender, one of the directors of the Psychology Institute of the University of Freiburg, Dr. F. Karger, a staff physicist at the Max Planck Institute for Plasmaphysics near Munich, and Dr. G. Zicha of the Munich Technical University. The sophisticated equipment they brought with them to investigate the case ruled out any trickery. It also ruled out any type of external electronic, magnetic, ultrasonic or infrasonic interference as an explanation. What had originally appeared to be caused by an electrical overload in the wiring system now turned out to be attributable to equally inexplicable random short-duration bursts of *nonelectrical* kinetic energy that physically smashed lamp bulbs (the filaments were still intact), tripped automatic fuses and played games with the telephone, the pictures and the filing cabinets.

Bender established that the phenomena seemed to focus around the person of an eighteen-year-old secretary, Annemarie S., who was at the time employed at the office. When she was subsequently dismissed, the phenomena ceased, suggesting again, as in the case of the Drummer of Tedworth, that a human agent was somehow responsible for the disturbances.[6]

Parapsychologists like Dr. Bender who have made a study of the poltergeist phenomenon now tend to attribute it to recurrent spontaneous psychokinesis (usually abbreviated to the initials RSPK) of one of the witnesses rather than to the machinations of malignant spirits.

Another frequently made observation in poltergeist cases is the emotionally violent atmosphere in which they often make their appearance. Often the suspected agent is discovered to be repressing strong feelings of hostility, rage, a sense of injustice, frustrated sexuality and so on, pointing again to the use of psi to service a deep-seated psychological need, in this instance to let off steam. Sometimes the hostility is reciprocated within a family context, which may in some way serve to add fuel to the phenomena.

Often, too, poltergeist agents appear to be more conscious than they let on as to who is responsible for the troublesome activity. Rarely, however, do they become entirely conscious of their own pronounced PK talents. Those who do tend to find a way of putting them to work, sometimes by rationalizing them to themselves as powers given by spirits (or, these days, given by the inhabitants of UFO's or agents of interstellar civilizations, it is often claimed).

PHYSICAL MEDIUMSHIP AND PK

When Spiritualism came into prominence as a religion during the nineteenth century, reports of objects flying about the séance room or mysteriously appearing and disappearing became something of a commonplace. Many if not most of them were probably due to a combination of fraud on the part of the mediums and wishful thinking on the part of the sitters. The need to establish evidence for postmortem survival was particularly strong then, because of the failure of organized religion to provide convincing and reassuring answers as it once had. This had been one of the chief motivations for the founding of the SPR. Such séance-room phenomena were generally attributed to the powers of the spirits of the dead, who were thought to use the body of the entranced medium as a sort of psychic telephone to the world of the living.

Not all mediums were fakes, however. Daniel Dunglas Home, born in 1833, a naturalized American medium popular with European royalty for his spectacular displays of séance phenomena, had a highly impressive record. Apparently he used to transform the Tuileries in Paris into a "regular witches' Sabbath," according to the account given by Princess Metternich, wife of the Austrian ambassador. In Home's presence massive pieces of furniture would rock violently in broad daylight and armchairs fly from one end of the room to the other "as if driven by a hurricane." [7]

Eusapia Palladino, an Italian medium who made her debut some fifty years after Home, caused a similar sensation with her feats of levitation and poltergeist activity, which were witnessed by a score of scientists, including both Curies.[8] Tables would levitate, raps and bangs be heard, inexplicable breezes felt and seen to billow curtains, mysterious lights illuminate the room and so on. Although hard scientific evidence for these mediums' capabilities is extremely poor by today's standards, the repeated pattern of inexplicable events that occurred during those experiments in which possibilities for cheating were precluded is significant. Eusapia, for one, was shown to have resorted to tricks time and again if and when she got the chance and wanted to bolster her performance. As is the case with many mediums, the need to impress or please her sitters seems to have been of considerable importance to her. Her attempts to cheat, however, were naive, obvious and readily detectable when she was made to perform under laboratory conditions. And when normal and possibly easier means of producing PK phenomena (that is, by cheating) were denied her, her paranormal powers would take over. Tables would rise, objects would sail around the room, fabrics would billow in mysterious, undetectable winds. The phenomena that Home, Palladino and others like them produced sound so like those produced by poltergeists as to be apparently closely related, if not one and the same thing.

Luckily for today's parapsychologist, although of extreme rarity, dramatic PK powers are not a thing of the past. Nina S. Kulagina, a woman with capabilities apparently similar to Palladino's, is being studied by Dr. G. A. Sergeev, a neuro-physiologist from Leningrad University. His work concerns what Soviet researchers call bioenergetic activity, the Russian term most nearly equivalent to our psychokinesis. Inanimate objects are reported to come to life and move about in Kulagina's presence in the time-honored way, a claim that has been demonstrated fairly persuasively on film recently.[9]

Uri Geller, a young Israeli sensitive, is another of today's candidates for PK stardom, although whether his talents lie in the area of psi or prestidigitation is still a matter of debate among parapsychologists. Like Kulagina, Geller has been filmed doing his PK thing, in his case bending or breaking small metal objects like keys and rings, allegedly by paranormal means.[10]

WHAT IS THE PK POWER?

Whether we call the PK effect bioenergy, as the Soviets do, or psychokinesis doesn't really help us to any further understanding of the riddle itself. We are still faced with the question: What is this force? Or to rephrase it more scientifically perhaps: What is happening when we see PK being exercised? In the case of most forces, we infer their existence by observing the movement of measurable objects or particles. When we see these things behaving strangely, in a manner contrary to their usual behavior, we say they are being acted on by a force. This goes for PK as much as it does for electromagnetism. What PK *is* may always remain a philosophical question in the same way as the nature of electrical charge has, or, when it comes to that, the nature of matter. From the standpoint of today's operational science, what PK *does*, and in how many ways, and how we start it or stop it, become the first questions to ask. How objects flying around the room fit into the currently accepted ideas about how electricity, magnetism, light and gravitation all hang together comes later.

Using the evidence of cases he has investigated, W. G. Roll suggests that poltergeist activity represents a conversion of his hypothesized psi field into kinetic energy. Energy is not a tangible substance (although paradoxically it possesses mass) but rather a shorthand term used by physicists to explain an object's or a particle's observed movement (kinetic energy) or its inclination to that movement (potential energy). In a neatly self-contained system an object's inclination to movement will always balance its resultant movement (once it gets going, so to speak). In the language of physics its potential energy is said to be exactly convertible to kinetic energy and vice versa—this is basically what Newton's Law of Conservation of Energy says.

What Roll seems to be suggesting is that the potential energy contained in the poltergeist agent's psi field is converted into kinetic energy around the various objects within the field's range, which the agent, for whatever psychological reason, zeroes in on. The effect of this is to set them flying about the room. Experiments conducted on Palladino by the Curies and others in Paris indicated that at the moment of the levitation of a table, although it was not observedly in contact with the medium, her weight as registered on a scale increased by the weight of the table, indicating a *mass loss* in the object equivalent to a *mass gain* in Palladino. Palladino was also frequently observed to tense her muscles spasmodically during or just prior to the PK occurrences.

Taking these two observations together—the medium's mass gain and muscle compression—and using Roll's psi-field hypothesis, we can concoct a theory that nicely compares with the classic example given by many physics textbooks for the conversion process of kinetic to potential energy. This says that when we compress a steel spring we are using kinetic energy to move the electrons of the metal into closer proximity. This sets up a strain in the metal (potential energy) owing to the electrons' natural tendency to repel one another. It has also been observed that we *add* to the spring's mass in this way. If the strain on the metal becomes intolerable, the electronic repulsion (potential energy) finally asserts itself, and the spring snaps back, sending whatever has been compressing it flying (kinetic energy).

In Palladino's case we may have a similar situation in biological terms. The medium spasmodically compresses her muscles (like a compressing spring), kinetic energy becomes potential energy registered in her psi field, and as a consequence her actual mass registers an increase. Her psi field now interacts with the psi field of the table. The potential energy seeking release converts to kinetic energy, which is registered physically as knocks, raps and finally movement. The movement becomes an upward one once the mass *increase* of Palladino has equaled the mass *decrease* of the table, causing it to float about.

In the instance of unconsciously produced poltergeist phenomena, Roll noted that objects distant from the suspected agent often moved farther than those close at hand, leading him to attribute a vortical shape to the field.[11] But at what level does the conversion from psi field to physical effect take place, one wonders? The molecular? The atomic? Dr. Bender and his colleagues found that the Rosenheim poltergeist showed no electromagnetic properties: What they recorded were simply bursts of inexplicable kinetic force. Is there, then, a powerful interaction at work in our lives of which we know nothing? It's hard to see how our trusty neutrinos could be directly responsible for this type of commotion by themselves, for by all accounts they have very little reactive tendency with matter.

Maybe the mischievous force is that of gravity itself. A helpful concept introduced to physics by Einstein was that space itself is bent around matter. Owing to this curvature, objects close to one another tend to "slip downhill" toward each other, a phenomenon we see and interpret as the force of gravity. As poltergeist activity has been seen to focus around specific objects as well as people, maybe they can be said to have been in some way polarized—or should we say "gravitized"?—by the unconscious agent. Perhaps the agent has in some as yet unexplainable way bent the space around him or her. When the objects subsequently fly about the room, are they, perhaps, in Einsteinian terms, simply slipping downhill? This would go part of the way to explain the slow, rather lazy movements of poltergeist-thrown objects sometimes noted. During both Palladino's and Home's séances small objects were observed to creep up the side of, or hop on top of, levitating tables as if drawn by some attracting force. Similarly, in Home's presence the flames of tilted, levitated candles were seen to discon-certingly retain their perpendicularity to the candle, another indication of a disruption of the normal gravitational field.

Needless to say, theories of gravitational warping and mass swapping like these can only be considered wildly speculative and, as such, useful only from the point of view of our psychological rationales. There are probably any number of undetected principles at work in the universe that could be responsible for the phenomena. Whatever does turn out to be responsible, however, it will have to be something that can effectively play games with gravity and perhaps even interfere with the electronic or nuclear forces that hold matter together, if we accept accounts of objects passing through walls and such other major physical undertakings.

BIOLOGICAL RAYS

If poltergeists and séance-room stunts represent extreme cases of PK activity, are there lesser manifestations of the same power that you or I could demonstrate?

De Rochas and Baraduc, two nineteenth-century researchers we encountered in Chapter Seven, theorized that the human body gives off biologically generated power that could be used to cause various psychic phenomena like Palladino's levitation and poltergeist tricks. They were not the first to propose the idea, however. Anton Mesmer, the discoverer of hypnotism, popularized the notion during the eighteenth century, and Baron Karl von Reichenbach, the nineteenth-century inventor of creosote, spent a large portion of his life and fortune experimenting with this hypothetical energy, which he claimed was given off by, and perceivable by, sensitives. He termed it (rather appropriately, one feels) "Od" force. His researches tended to support the belief widely held among spiritualists at the time that the medium and sometimes the sitters contributed power from their own bodies that was used by the spirits to produce physical phenomena, levitation, materialization and dematerialization of small objects, mysterious lights, scents, sounds and so on.

Baraduc and his fellow researchers experimented with a

variety of gadgets that supposedly showed the action of this human "neuricity," as he called it. All of them employed paper or straw pointers mounted on spindles or needles suspended on fine threads—both types of apparatus being placed under a glass bell jar to protect them from stray air currents. When the pointers of such fluid motors—biometers, sthenometers or magnetometers, as they were variously called—were seen to spin at the approach of the medium's hand, it was taken as an evident sign of the externalized power streaming from his or her fingertips.

However, if you construct a simple sthenometer for yourself by sticking a needle upright into a cork, balancing a little paper star on its point so that it spins freely and covering the entire arrangement with an upended mayonnaise jar, you can sometimes get the star to spin very effectively on warm, dry days by shuffling your feet on the carpet and holding your hand alongside the jar. (See Figure 10.) The explanation, of course, is

Figure 10. Homemade Sthenometer

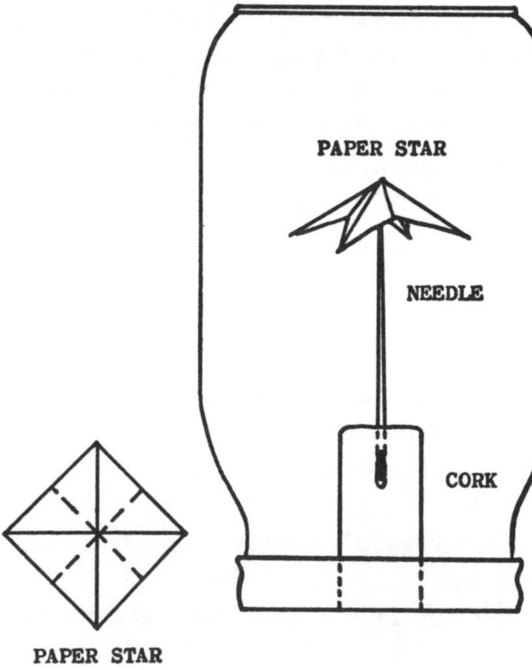

PAPER STAR

NEEDLE

CORK

PAPER STAR

static electricity, not any type of mysterious biological energy. Static electricity and heat radiation may have been the explanation for the successful operation of such gadgets most of the time, although this need not always have been the case. Instances of genuine localized poltergeist power like that apparently demonstrated by Kulagina might well have edged in alongside.

DEMONSTRATING PK FOR YOURSELF

Obviously, then, when using such crude devices it is difficult for us to distinguish between any genuine PK abilities we might possess and the quirks of static electricity and heat radiation. There are two reliable experiments, however, that can be performed in the home to demonstrate the presence or absence in us of this mysterious power: Rhine's PK experiments with dice and PK tests on plants. Strangely enough, parapsychologists were not the first to observe the mind's effect in these two areas. As far back as the sixteenth century Francis Bacon, the philosopher-statesman, noted that the power believed by many of his contemporary savants to reside in the human imagination could best be tested "upon things that have the lightest and easiest motions . . . as upon the sudden fading, or lively coming up of herbs; or upon their bending one way or other . . . or upon the casting of dice." [12] There's nothing new under the sun, apparently, even in parapsychology!

HOW TO CONDUCT A PK EXPERIMENT WITH DICE

Basically all you need for this type of test is a couple of regular numbered dice, an empty coffee can or similar container to shake them in, and a flat surface with a backstop, such as a table covered with a blanket set against a wall.

The object of the exercise is to try to influence the dice to fall with a certain number uppermost, the way a craps shooter who feels he has power over the dice does. Ideally you should avoid using the 6 face as a target, for this one is lighter than the other five (there are six little hollows in it), and theoretically at least it will be biased to fall uppermost. For this type of simple home experiment, however, you can forget about such restrictions.

Parapsychologists consider a run of thirty-six throws to be a suitable basis for PK evaluation. You can split this into six runs of six if you wish, "willing" a different die face in each run. Simply shake the dice in the can and roll them so that they bounce off the backstop.

METHODS OF "WILLING"

How, exactly, does one best will a side of a die to fall uppermost? It's a question that still concerns psi researchers. Francis Bacon considered that the answer lay in the exercise of the imagination, although he never really explained what he understood by the word. Presumably he meant a combination of visualization and expectation. Rex Stanford of the University of Virginia School of Medicine, whose psychic "luck" theory we touched on in Chapter Two, performed a series of PK experiments recently to test the effectiveness of two different approaches to this problem.[13] In half his experiments, Stanford's subjects were instructed to visualize vividly the die turning up the agreed-upon face at the end of its roll. In the other half, the subjects were made to "free associate" to the agreed-upon die face for two minutes previously; that is, to tell the experimenter every word, concept or thought that entered their heads when thinking about the number on the die face. Then they were instructed to put the entire matter out of their minds while the experiment proceeded by reading a book, going for a walk, whatever they liked. In this way Stanford hoped to alert the *unconscious* areas of their minds to the PK task rather than the *conscious* parts as the visualization method would do. The PK task would be unconscious because they had forgotten about it, or at least pushed it out of their immediate conscious awareness. Stanford's reason for trying this approach was as follows:

In the same way that ESP signals are often most effectively hooked during periods of latency when we are concentrating on something else—for instance, the next card in the deck—so it apparently is with PK, or at least with RSPK. Spontaneous outbursts of poltergeist activity have a knack of occurring at the very moment that the witnesses' attentions are turned elsewhere. Similarly, the masquerade of spirit control at a séance has been interpreted by some parapsychologists as a device to allow the phenomena to occur freely without intervention from the medium's conscious mind; a means, in effect, of tying up and neutralizing his or her reasoning process similar to knot tying and rosary chanting. This "watched-kettle-never-boils" idea crops up again and again in parapsychology, as we have seen. It seems to point to a fundamental factor of some sort in the psi process, a factor that carries intriguing echoes of the Either/Or-but-Not-Both behavior physicists see exhibited by an elementary particle, whereby the very act of *observing* one alters its essential nature. Maybe a conscious thought (or an automatism or a poltergeist trick, for that matter) always represents the end of a psi-field transaction, completing the circuit, as it were, leaving no energy at large for any more psychic fun-and-games? Hence the observed unconsciousness of the psi process.

The results of Stanford's experiment suggested that those subjects who tended on the whole to think in concrete visual images (as opposed to intellectual abstractions) scored highest with the visualization technique. He also noted that all his subjects, regardless of the way they thought, scored higher on die faces that had triggered off a good flow of associations for them—an observation that happens to accord well with W. G. Roll's theory touched on in Chapter Five about idea association and the part it plays in the phenomenon of psychometry. This psi *focusing effect*, as it has now come to be known among parapsychologists, seems therefore to be applicable to both ESP and PK, still further support for Rhine's theory that ESP and PK are two sides of the same psi coin.

Name: John Doe **Date:** 9/19/74

Type of test: PK (dice)

TARGET FACE	1	2	3	4	5	6
	3 2②	6 4	2④	④ 1	3 5	⑥
	4 ①3	1③	1 1	3 4	2 1	2
	① 5 6	5 6	6 5	2 2	6 1	1
	6 2②	1 1	2 3	④ 6	⑤⑥	5
	2 3 4	5 5	2 5	1 6	3 3	⑥
	3 3 6	②2	③6	2⑤	2⑥	5
TOTAL	2	3	2	3	2	4

Figure 11. PK Dice Test Record Sheet

METHODS OF PSI FOCUSING

Bearing these observations in mind, before conducting your dice experiment, focus your psi field on the die faces by taking a piece of paper and spending a minute or two looking at each die face, jotting down those things the number conjures up in your mind: birthdays, house numbers, telephone numbers, rhymes, days of the week, traumatic incidents, words, whatever. Keep the amount of time you spend on each die face uniform. This is most important.

Then add up the words for each die face to see which ones have elicited the most responses. These are the best target faces for you to concentrate on, for they are the ones with which you have the largest built-in psychological rapport.

Experiment with both "visualization" and "forgetting" techniques to see which gives you the highest score.

CHECKING YOUR RESULTS

Note your results down on a record sheet (see Figure 11), and when you have completed your runs, check for PK indications against the following rule-of-thumb table.

EVALUATION SCALE

Number of Runs of 6 Throws Each	Chance Expectation	PK Suggestive *(odds 20 to 1)*	PK Significant *(odds 100 to 1)*
6	12 hits	17 or 7 hits	18 and over; or 6 or under
12	24 hits	30–31; or 17–18 hits	32 and over; or 16 or under
24	48 hits	57–58; or 38–39 hits	59 and over; or 37 or under
36	72 hits	83–85; or 59–61 hits	86 and over; or 58 or under

Well, does your psi emerge as PK, or not? Don't feel too bad if it doesn't. As with psi missing in your ESP tests, spectacularly negative scores may indicate that you are using your PK to scramble the results rather than fit in with the experimental goal, possibly for a variety of psychological reasons—not the least of which may be the revolt of your own common sense at the idea of the power of mind over matter.

HOW TO CONDUCT A PK EXPERIMENT
WITH PLANTS

We all know people who have a "green thumb," who have something about them that seems to cause any plants they take care of to grow and bloom luxuriantly. Back in the early 1950's Rhine had his attention drawn to this phenomenon as a possible instance of PK exercised by the gardener over his plants.[14] In 1963 Bernard Grad, a biochemist working at McGill University in Montreal, followed up on this suggestion while he was testing the powers of Oskar Estebany, a well-known spiritual healer. Instead of using human targets, Grad put the healer to work in the area of plant growth. His experimental results showed that some type of beneficent influence did in fact seem to be emanating from the healer and inducing more luxuriant growth in the plants he had tested.[15]

Dr. Grad went on to perform a further series of plant experiments, this time testing the influence of ordinary, supposedly nonpsychic, people instead of a healer. Two of his three subjects, moreover, were psychiatric patients suffering from symptoms of depression. Significantly, the single normal subject attained the most positive results and produced strong evidence that her "blessed" plants did better than the "unblessed." The mentally depressed subjects scored less well in a proportion that appeared to tally with the seriousness of their conditions, a finding that fits in well with our rationale concerning positive and negative mental attitudes and how they may orient our unconscious use of psi.[16]

Our experiment is based upon those of Dr. Grad and Dr. and Mrs. Paul Vasse, the researchers who first drew Rhine's attention to plant PK in the 1950's. According to our rationale, our psi field can not only adhere to objects but does so best when fixed by strong emotions. In the following experiment we shall see if life processes in germinating seeds can be accelerated or inhibited by the emotionally charged psi field associated with the water used to irrigate them. Although we consider it a PK experiment here, the plant test does bring out how arbitrary and thin the dividing line between the twin areas of PK and ESP can often be. As usual, it boils down to a question of whose point of view you are looking at the phenomenon from: the psychologist's or the physicist's. From the psychologist's viewpoint we are performing an experiment in ESP, psychometrically imprinting the water with our emotions. From the physicist's we are doing a PK experiment, radiating the water with biological emanations of some sort. The factor common to both viewpoints is the imprinting or radiating process and *how* whatever it is that is imprinted or radiated then affects what it comes in contact with. ESP or PK; emotions or emanations? Maybe one day we'll discover a way to prove they're really different aspects of the same thing.

METHOD

1. Fill three identical flowerpots with potting mix taken from the same bag. In each pot plant an identical number of identical seeds—beans sold at groceries for home sprouting are ideal, but any type of quickly germinating garden seed will do. Place all three pots in saucers in a position that as nearly as possible allows them to receive the maximum (and equal) amount of light and shelter—possibly on a sunny windowsill. Label one pot A, the other B, the third C. In laboratory language, pot C will be our control.

2. Now fill three large covered containers with water. (The plastic jugs distilled water is sold in are fine for this.) Label them A, B and C. Place both your hands around container A and for fifteen minutes pretend you can feel energy radiating from them through the container into the water. If you think about it hard enough you will begin to feel your pulse beating in each finger. Pretend that each pulsebeat sends a wave of warm energy into the water. Pretend also that each energy wave carries with it the power to promote healthy growth, to encourage and develop life

in all its forms, animal or vegetable. Visualize lush tropical jungles and equatorial rain forests where plants run riot; or great horticultural greenhouses, vast palaces peopled by exotic plants—orchids and hanging mosses and tree ferns. Allow your imagination a field day. Conjure up in your imagination the odor of loam and peat moss. Feel benevolent toward plants in general, and pretend you are injecting your benevolence into the water. Recall how plants are our main food source, how they keep us alive. Imagine yourself talking to them like pets or tiny children, encouraging them and praising them. Pretend the concentrated force of your life-giving imagination is pouring into the water and charging it like a battery.

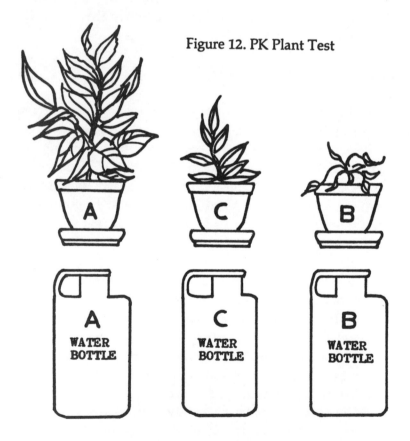

Figure 12. PK Plant Test

3. Now repeat the process with water container B, but this time give the water *negative* suggestions and use antiplant visualizations. Feel your hands radiating cold, withering energy, a power to bind and stunt and inhibit. Visualize a barren wilderness where no plants grow—deserts, rocks, the lunar landscape, city asphalt or polluted industrial waste. Again put your imagination to work, this time conjuring up an antiplant environment, seeing the seeds sending up withered, stunted growths or none at all, hearing yourself despising them, hating them, putting them down as miserable and unwanted weeds. Remember how you feel about stinging nettles and poison ivy!

4. Leave the water in container C exactly "as is." Water the seeds in the pots with a little of the water from their respective containers at the same time twice a day: pot A from container A, pot B from container B, pot C from container C. (See Figure 12.)

CHECKING YOUR RESULTS

Ideally, if the experiment is a success and you do find you have localized PK (literally) at your fingertips, pot A should begin to flourish first, pot C next, pot B last. Ideally, that is. You may find, however, that pot B paradoxically produces as luxurious growth as A, or pot C more than either! Why should this be? Remember psi missing? If PK is influencing the results, it may not be as responsive to our conscious will as we would like. Hence, when we think we are "radiating" the water in container B with life-inhibiting thoughts, we may be unconsciously resisting this deliberate herbicide (especially if we are averse to killing) and giving out quite contrary radiations. Or conversely, we may have a possibly unconscious lack of sympathy or even dislike for plants, or maybe a psychological bent (remember Grad's depressed subjects?) that is simply not in tune with plant growing. Any of these factors could, theoretically at least, put a jinx on our radiations.

The deciding factor as to the presence or absence of PK is the untreated control pot C, for this represents the norm. Whether our PK is playing along with our mental suggestions or not, if it *is* tipping the balance one way or the other, aiding growth or inhibiting it, we may get an indication of the fact by comparing the results of pots A and B with pot C, noting any unusual growth or lack of it.

NINE

Using PK in Daily Life

THE NEED FOR AN APPROPRIATE CHANNEL

Unless we happen to be born with pronounced PK powers, like D. D. Home or Palladino, most of us show only rudimentary signs, if any, of PK "spill" in our daily lives. Like ESP, whose other face it seems to be, PK may turn out to be part of our biological life-support equipment, exhibiting itself only in pronounced forms like poltergeist pranks under conditions of abnormal stress, illness or in people with distinctive psychological constitutions. If PK is the motor aspect of ESP, it undoubtedly is there all the time in any case, working away under the surface, prompting, nudging, tipping the scales of events one way or another. Like ESP, PK may well respond to efforts to develop it, *provided* we choose an area or channel compatible with its natural role in our lives. Two such channels could well be the practice of petitionary or intercessory prayer and the more specific one of spiritual or psychic healing.

Since we have already touched on the psi aspects of prayer under the heading of "ESP Broadcasting" in Chapter Four, we shall be concentrating here on the second channel, paranormal healing, although the general principles of psi broadcasting seem to hold true for both areas. One is merely a more specific application than the other.

When we survey the field of paranormal healing, a number

of different forms, both religious and nonreligious, present themselves for consideration. Most of them overlap to such an extent that it becomes fairly apparent that, given the phenomenon of psi, the differences of approach could well be said to stem from differences of *rationale* rather than anything intrinsic to the processes themselves. This is the point of view we will be adopting here. We shall assume that, in all cases, paranormal diagnosis and healing, if and when they occur, are a result of psi-field interaction, not the intervention of supernatural entities.

PK AND PARANORMAL HEALING

For the purposes of this chapter, therefore, we shall divide psi healing into three categories:

Type 1 PK BROADCASTING

In view of the difficulty of distinguishing between ESP and PK, especially when it becomes a question of psi influence exerted over the human organism, we can consider this similar or identical to ESP broadcasting, if only for the sake of categorization. As we have seen, it could well be that the distinction between the two is entirely one of appearance: In ESP, brain consciousness is reacting to the psi field; in PK, *things* are, be they organic or inorganic. Roll has speculated that the normal attenuation of the psi field remains operative (the Inverse Two-fifths Law?) until such time as it becomes localized and converted to kinetic energy around physical objects (PK). It would be interesting to know if the corollary were true: namely, whether the reception of an ESP signal by one party in any way used it up, so to speak, precluding its reception by a second.

Although it is tempting to lump all paranormal healing under a general heading labeled telepathy plus psychosomatic effect, instances of healers apparently experiencing energy depletion as a consequence of their healing are indicative that actual energy transfer does sometimes occur.[1] Remembering the extraordinary mass transference registered between Eusapia Palladino and the table, this should not come as too much of a surprise to us. *What* type of energy is transferred becomes the question again. The ancient Chinese believed that the energy used by healers, *ch'i*, was the energy of life itself, which we normally extract from food and air. Was this simply an abstraction, a primitive way of expressing the metabolic processes of oxygenation and deoxygenation of the blood and the assimilation of food, or did it go farther than that? Inasmuch as *ch'i* was considered to work in principle like a siphon, lesser amounts automatically drawing on greater amounts until balance was achieved, the Chinese always insisted that the healer be in a more glowing state of health than his patient, lest the flow go the wrong way and the patient end up in an even worse state than before! [2]

Maybe we can borrow from the Chinese and state that the psi field of the healer expends itself (via the psi field of the patient) kinetically in the body of the patient. This activity is registered as an increase in the patient's power to metabolize and take care of his own psychophysiological problems or diseases; a bolstering of his powers to rally and to counter infection. If the healer's psi field meshes with the patient's psi field and converts to kinetic energy, the law of energy conservation indicates that the healer will experience a consequent energy loss equal to the gain in the patient, which is in fact what sometimes seems to happen.

When it takes place within a framework of religious beliefs, "broadcast" healing of this sort is often considered to occur as a result of intercessory prayer: that is, when the healer prays for the recovery of the patient. In some instances it is referred to as *absent healing*, owing to the fact that the subject's presence is not required by the healer. [3]

Type 2 LOCALIZED PK

In religious practice, the age-old rite of blessing, healing by touch or the "laying on of hands" would correspond to PK focused by means of touch or massage. "Psychic surgery," the alleged woundless rearrangement of interior tissue by PK, would also fall into this category. Healing by touch is practiced by both religious and nonreligious healers.

Type 3 PK BATTERIES

Healing obtained as a result of pilgrimages to shrines or places considered holy, the carrying of blessed objects and the eating of sacramental food would all fall under this heading. So also would the unorthodox form of healing known as radionics, an extension of the principle of psychometry. Here an object associated with the person who requires healing is used for purposes of diagnosis and treatment, similar to the way the psychometrist uses an object to link him with a missing person.

Shrines, sacraments, talismans and radionic objects become a little more rational when viewed in the light of the concept of an accompanying psi field built up or modified by the action of minds of worshipers, priests or healers attuned to the idea of healing. In this way the object or place could be considered a psi battery capable of conducting healing thoughts, emotions or whatever it is that constitutes psi energy into the psi field of the subject.

ELEMENTS INVOLVED IN PARANORMAL HEALING

The observation that gifted ESP sensitives can not only score well in PK tests but sometimes, like Gerard Croiset, find themselves capable of using their psi for paranormal healing, lends a certain amount of support to our theory of the reciprocal nature of these two phenomena. From the scattered references to their methods made by healers, we can piece together a composite technique that in essence seems to be no different from the basic technique used in ESP broadcasting. Although healers are even vaguer than sensitives about their modus operandi, it often appears to involve at least the following elements:

1. Mutual faith by healer and patient in the possibility of such healing.

2. A state of psychological *unconflictedness* in the healer, sometimes aided by rhythmic breathing exercises, prayer, or meditation.

3. A deeply felt sympathy by the healer for the patient.

4. Often, the laying on of hands.

5. A blanking of the healer's mind.

MUTUAL FAITH

As in all attempts to exercise psychic power consciously, faith in at least its *possibility* seems to be extremely important to clear away psi-negative blocks, if nothing else. This requirement usually applies to both healer and patient. An interesting sidelight is thrown on this faith factor by Sister M. Justa Smith, who combines the duties of a Franciscan nun with those of a research biochemist and chairman of the National Sciences Concentration at Rosary Hill College in Buffalo. At a forum sponsored by the Association for Humanistic Psychology in 1972, Dr. Smith noted the recent case of a doctor curing a patient of a disease with a medically worthless placebo that both he and the patient at the time mistakenly believed to be a drug of proven efficacy. Had their combined faiths somehow set up a healing "faith circuit," Dr. Smith wondered?

Recently Dr. Frederick J. Evans of the University of Pennsylvania reported corroborative evidence for this type of phenomenon to a convention of the American Psychosomatic Society held in Philadelphia. Thirty-six percent of the patients he had studied reported significant pain relief after taking worthless placebos—in whose effectiveness both the patient and the doctor believed at the time. Obviously the healing did not derive from the medicinally worthless substance, so perhaps it somehow came from the combined mental attitudes of the doctor and his patient. Could it be, then, that many physicians use paranormal healing power to effect cures from time to time without their being aware of the fact? It's an intriguing thought.

PSYCHOLOGICAL UNCONFLICTEDNESS

It has often been recommended that the healer use breathing exercises as a preliminary to therapy. Concepts of energy intake similar to those of Oriental philosophy, *prana* or *ch'i*, are usually offered as rationales for the practice. Chinese healers do in fact use deliberate rhythmic breathing in their craft, apparently as much to help them identify with their patient as to draw in *ch'i*. The healer is instructed to inhale deeply, filling his abdomen three inches below the navel with air. The actual breathing rhythm is to be made to correspond to that of the patient.[4]

A secondary and more obvious benefit to be obtained from deep breathing is its ability to help you to relax, as Eileen Garrett stated.[5] Mrs. Garrett also claimed deep breathing enabled her to pull herself together or, to put it a little more precisely, to reach that condition of *unconflictedness* so necessary for the exercise of psi. Apropos of unconflictedness, even if we do not accept the dogma that generally accompanies religious rationales for psi, a certain amount of practical parapsychological advice may be contained in the Christian Church's teaching about prayer or, as we term it here, psi broadcasting. The necessity for a state of psychological unconflictedness before prayer will work is a case in point. The two-thousand-year-old advice to the petitioner to *believe* that his infringements on other people's rights are pardoned, coupled with the instruction to abandon his own resentment of other people's infringements on *his* rights, may well represent an attempt to reach such a state of unconflictedness. Similarly, the deliberate attempt by modern petitioners of Divine Grace to identify themselves mentally with a transcendant force—whether they choose to call it God, Jesus, the Buddha, their guru, or depersonalize it as a Cosmic Mind—may again prove to be a useful psychological trick to help them, like mediums, to clear the board of subjective psychological blocks and produce a state of unconflictedness that allows their psi fields unimpeded play.

THE EMOTIONAL LINK

Like ESP, paranormal healing seems to require some genuine sympathetic feeling on the part of the healer for his patient; a feeling usually described as empathy, pity, compassion or love. If psi healing does function in a way similar to ESP, then this emotion may well play the part of a hook or focusing device. Not only must the healer feel genuinely sorry for the patient, but he must to some degree be able to identify with him. Dr. Bernard Grad believes that such attitudes of compassion and love not only promote paranormal healing but continually operate between mother and child or husband and wife, generally favoring growth and development. Where the reverse is true, maybe we can look for those destructive runs of "bad luck" and, in pronounced cases, incidences of poltergeist tricks?

THE LAYING ON OF HANDS

The ancient practice of healing by touch is at least as old as the Bible and is employed to this day as an adjunct to psychic healing of the localized-PK or PK-battery varieties.

Four possible explanations could account for its efficacy:

1. It acts out dramatically the transmission of healing power.

2. It soothes the patient by its psychological significance, perhaps recalling the comforting touch of a parent.

3. It transmits some type of biologically generated power.

4. It acts as a *noncerebral* focusing device to enable both healer and patient to localize the sought-after psi-field effect.

THE BLANKED MIND

Perhaps all four explanations are true to some degree, although ancient Chinese healers advocated that the healer's mind be blanked and his attention focused only on his hands, which would seem to indicate the relative importance of theories 3 and 4, but more especially 4. The blanked-mind requirement seems particularly significant in view of what we have learned about the phenomenon of latency in psi processes. Emptying our conscious minds and letting our hands do the thinking for us is, after all, just another way of describing manual automatism such as we use in pendulum swinging or table tilting.

There are a number of simple exercises we can employ to cultivate this awareness of our hands. Most of us possess it to some degree, particularly those whose jobs involve working with their hands. The problem really seems to boil down to a matter of learning how to switch this unthinking awareness on and off when we need it.

HAND-SENSITIZATION EXERCISES

EXERCISE A

1. Sit comfortably with your hands in your lap.
2. Observe them carefully for a minute or two.
3. Be aware of the blood pulsing through them.
4. Now, concentrate your attention on the fingers, particularly the fingertips. You will become aware of a curious tingling feeling there. This is simply the combined effort of your pulse and the nerves on the surface of the skin responding to your attention.
5. Now, learn to reproduce this tingle without looking at your fingers. You can do this at any time of the day when you think of it. Judge yourself proficient when you can instantly switch on the tingle full force.

EXERCISE B

Try the old dowser's trick of holding your hands above household energy sources such as lighted lamps or running electrical machines (e.g., an electric clock) and seeing what type of sensation you can elicit in your hands. Dowsers would say you were reacting to the electromagnetic radiation, although most psychologists and many parapsychologists would say the effect is due to simple autosuggestion. Whatever the reason, it is the tingle we're after. According to our rationale, it will enable us to localize *mindlessly* the psi effect in the same way that a pendulum does.

PRACTICING HEALING

Of the five elements involved in healing (see page 145), items 2 and 5 are the only ones you can really practice on your own, without the presence of an actual subject. Items 1 and 3, your faith and sympathy, are up to your psychological constitution. Either you feel them at the time of healing or you don't!

Once you are satisfied as to your ability to call up in yourself a state of mental unconflictedness and have the knack of letting your hands take over, you are probably ready to begin your first attempt. Touch the patient on or near the affected spot or, alternatively, hold your hands four to six inches above it, focusing as much of your awareness as you can in the fingertips and palms. After a minute or two, if your psi does favor this type of channeling, your patient may begin to feel a corresponding tingle or warmth at or near the point of contact. In extreme cases this has been described as growing to a throbbing sensation that may be felt over a large area of the body. (Physical science gives the lie to the objectivity of the sensation: No actual temperature rise has been recorded in such instances, leading one to suspect that, as with the hand-sensitization exercises, the peculiar sensation is a result of the patient's attention being drawn to the area's nerve and pulse activity.) Go on the simpleminded assumption that the patient's own body knows instinctively how to take care of itself. All you are doing is lending it a little energy to do this via your interlocking psi fields.

Don't be ambitious to begin with. Remember, not everyone's psi will choose healing as its channel. Try your powers on simple ailments at first, like tension headaches and sprains. If you do have a penchant for healing, you'll probably soon find out. For generalized conditions like sleeplessness, depression, exhaustion, colds and fevers, concentrate your hands' attention on the head, the neck and the facial areas of the patient. Suspecting what we do about the transmissibility of the psi field, try using your hands to charge medicines, salves and bandages before using them, and see if this improves their effectiveness in any way.

One last thing: Never allow your healing to dissuade you from making regular visits to the doctor. Nor should you ever discourage people from consulting a physician on the strength of your or others' healing sessions. As with all psi powers, full control seems a long way off yet. Even the greatest healers with the highest numbers of successes are not sure of what is going on all the time, or even half the time, for that matter.[6] Remember, too, that psi seems always to make use of our own psychophysiological processes to express itself. When used in a healing channel, it seems to be stimulating the same defense mechanisms in our bodies that medicines do. Whereas medicines work from outside in, psi works from inside out. Lastly, we should never forget that the truly sympathetic and gifted physician may well be employing his psi as well as his normal therapy to heal us, whether he happens to know it or not.

TEN

On Seeing Ghosts

The observation that children are more sensitive to atmospheres than adults has become something of a truism in psychology. That such sensitivity may well extend beyond the recognized range of family relationships into the realm of the paranormal is not so well known. I experienced my first and only ghost when I was a small child, toward the end of World War II. As is frequently the case with ghost sightings, I cannot be absolutely sure it was not merely a vivid dream, save for the rather exceptional circumstances that were subsequently shown to have surrounded it. I will describe the encounter in some detail, as it brings out several rather important points about the nature of ghosts.

My parents, glad to have a respite from the oppressive terror of the London blitz, had taken me to vacation at a friend's house in Lincolnshire. The house itself, an Elizabethan manor named Thorpe Hall, happens to be one of the most famous haunted houses in England, although neither of my parents knew it at the time. The owner of the house was absent during the major portion of my parents' stay, and the day in question was the housekeeper's day off. Both my parents were sunning themselves on the lawn after lunch, and I had been left upstairs in the empty house for my afternoon nap. I was fairly used to my parents bringing friends of theirs into my room to visit me, so when I saw the woman in the green dress standing beside my bed I greeted her matter-of-factly and asked if it was time for me to get up. Unfortunately I don't remember if I received any reply.

When subsequently, rather insistently, I asked my parents who my visitor in the long green dress had been, they were mystified and ascribed the incident to a vivid dream. It was only later that they learned of the legend of the Green Lady, the daughter of a Spanish grandee, whose ghost is supposed to walk the corridors of Thorpe Hall, her faithless English lover's old home. Her phantom has been seen repeatedly since the time of the Spanish Armada—a woman in a long green dress moving sadly about the house and grounds.

My mild tale is, of course, unspectacular when viewed beside the many hair-raising tales of ghost encounters that fill the annals of psychic research.[1] But it does serve to illustrate several important points: first, that ghosts are not necessarily sinister; second, that they do not have to appear at night; third, that they can be mistaken for real people; fourth, that they can appear to children; fifth, that they can appear even to those who do not believe in them.

Romantic as the notion of unquiet spirits may be, parapsychologists have a rather different explanation for ghostly phenomena. We saw earlier how sensitives are often able to read an object for its emotional associations. In cases of haunting we seem to have instances of psychometry being performed on a large scale. Here it is the location itself that becomes an object of terrific emotional imprinting, developing a psi field like a wound-up spring. Someone sufficiently sensitive—or possessed with sufficient PK ability in the case of a chain-clanking ghost —to react to this charged psi field sets off the haunting.

In the case of visual appearances the haunting is a hallucination perceived by the brain of the sensitive. My eyes *saw* the Green Lady, although there was probably nothing physically there. The seeing, however, was sufficiently real and undream-like for me to mistake it for reality: no theatrical shroud or semitransparency here. By all accounts, unless the ghost does something extraordinary like wearing obviously outlandish clothes or walking through a wall, a visual experience of a phantom is often difficult to differentiate from a visual experience of a real person. In both cases our brains are presenting us with solid-looking visual images. It's possible, then, that we have all at some time in our lives seen ghosts and never known it, in the same way that we have all experienced general ESP and not known it!

Why ghosts appear sporadically and not continuously may well have to do with the state of mind of the sensitive. Only when certain as-yet-unspecifiable psychological conditions are realized—when he is sufficiently sleepy, off guard, stimulated, dissociated or whatever—will the cogs mesh and the "haunting spring" unwind. Why does not the repeated seeing of the ghost exhaust the energy of the psi imprint causing it? Possibly for the same reason the turning of a waterwheel does not exhaust the energy of the waterfall. The water falls because of the shape of its location. A house becomes haunted when the shape of its psi field is twisted or bent by strong emotion. In the Green Lady's case, the original emotion may have been that of the lady herself or, more probably, that of the house's first owner. Old houses stand a better chance of being haunted than new simply because of the sheer quantity of tenants available to do the imprinting, although ancient castles do not by any means hold a monopoly on the phenomenon. A surprising number of houses built within the last fifty years in Hollywood, for example, have acquired hair-raising ghostly reputations.

EXPLORING HAUNTED HOUSES

When you do take time to develop your psi awareness, you of course open up the whole area of ghosts and hauntings as a fruitful field for personal exploration. Ghost hunting is a time-consuming operation but can be thrilling fun if you have the nerve for it.

To the psychic researcher, finding a genuine ghost is on a par with finding a pearl in your oyster: an extremely rare experience to be treasured always. Needless to say, the sentiment is not one universally shared. When a family discovers they are sharing their house with a ghost, the first impulse is to have it exorcised as soon as possible. It is on this basis that parapsychologists often gain access to genuine hauntings, although the families frequently end up resenting their presence—if and when it becomes apparent, as it usually does, that they are less interested in defusing the ghost than encouraging it for their own investigative purposes. Obviously, if you do happen to hear about a local haunting and get the opportunity to investigate it, it is uncool to show too much enjoyment at the prospect of witnessing what to the owner of the house is probably a source of considerable emotional and possible financial distress.

In addition to conducting your initial investigation in a balanced and reassuring manner, you should also ask the tenants a few questions to establish the degree of plausibility of the alleged manifestations and perhaps save yourself and your friends a wasted trip.

QUESTIONS TO ASK

1. Where exactly do the disturbances occur (in which room, etc.)?

2. When do they occur?

3. How often? At regular intervals?

4. Do they ever happen when there is no one around? If the answer is "yes," it could indicate PK activity (chain clanking, raps, voices, defacement or movement of objects, etc.) or, alternatively, fraud. Remember, trickery can be unconscious sometimes, and often represents someone's attention-getting device.

5. Regarding this, ascertain whether there are children near

at hand. Could they have been responsible for faking the alleged phenomena?

6. What adults have experienced the phenomena? Do they have a history of psychic experiences? This can be a telling question from two points of view: (a) the witness may be predisposed to psychic activity and therefore possibly the agent responsible for triggering the haunting; or (b) he or she may simply be imagining it in order to bolster his or her beliefs in psychic marvels.

7. Has the ghostly activity ever been witnessed by some people in the room and not by others? This question will help to nail down the extent of the hallucinatory nature of the phenomena and also perhaps who the PK agents or sensitives in the household are.

8. Do the ghosts or images resemble living persons or events known to any of the witnesses? That is, could the haunting be an occurrence of a straightforward clairvoyant or telepathic hallucination?

9. Do the ghosts or images resemble persons or events from the past? Is there any evidence for this, such as history-book descriptions, photographs, old news clippings and so on?

10. Did the witnesses know about these historical people or events before they saw the ghost?

11. Does the house have a reputation for being haunted?

12. Did any of the witnesses know of this reputation when they saw the ghost? [2]

HOW TO GHOST HUNT

You will probably want to make your actual ghost foray in the company of like-minded friends. This is a good idea, as the additional points of view will help to corroborate impressions. In an area where hallucination plays such a large part, witnesses count for a lot. If they have worked at developing their psi powers too, so much the better.

Besides taking notebooks, plan also on having cameras with flash attachments and a tape recorder to collect hard evidence. If you hear sounds or see something that fails to show up on tape or film, you will have good reason to believe in a hallucinatory explanation of the phenomena—as opposed to a PK one. Of course, if you are doing your search in conjunction with a parapsychology group, you may have access to more elaborate detection equipment to bring along with you, such as photometers to register light changes or thermistors to measure temperature rises or drops. Automatic equipment is best, as ghostly phenomena, like psi in general, usually seem to occur when one's back is turned or when one is least expecting them.

If the previous history of haunting is of the poltergeist variety, you can place various target objects at strategic points in the hope that the force will oblige you by moving them. If your ghost has a record of visible appearances, arrange to set up mirrors at strategic points, too. The old belief that ghosts and supernatural entities do not cast a shadow or reflection may well derive from the nonreflectability of hallucinations. Actually this mirror trick may not always work, for experiments with hypnotically induced hallucinations have shown that a *really* resourceful hypnotic subject will even go so far as to provide a shadow for his hallucination. But by using mirrors, you can at least give your hallucinations a good run for their money!

You can also draw up a ground plan of the location you are investigating and provide each member of your party with a copy. Then, using vision or any other ESP technique you possess, you can scan the location for impressions in the same way that a dowser scans a locale for water. Mark your plans where you feel the focal points of the manifestations lie, and compare notes afterward.

You should also run through the following checklist, adapted for ghost hunting by Gertrude Schmeidler from Gough's Adjective Checklist, to try to determine the emotional *quality* of the impressions your group gets from this scanning:

active	dignified	mature
affectionate	distrustful	meek
aggressive	emotional	mischievous
alert	enterprising	noisy
aloof	fearful	obliging
anxious	forgiving	patient
apathetic	friendly	peaceable
arrogant	gentle	quiet
bitter	greedy	rigid
calm	headstrong	shy
changeable	helpful	stern
cold	humorous	strong
complaining	immature	submissive
confused	impatient	tolerant
contented	impulsive	trusting
cruel	independent	vindictive
demanding	irritable	warm
despondent	jolly	weak [3]
determined	leisurely	

Compare your results among yourselves now and note similarities. Of course this is by no means a conclusive test of the ghost's emotional nature. In the event of similarities you could well be simply picking up one another's own broadcast emotions, although the use of ground plans to localize the influences does help to narrow down the probabilities for this. It would be reasonable to assume that a feeling of menace consistently emanating from only one corner of a room indicated something peculiar about the area itself, which of course is one of the prime characteristics of a haunting.

Once you have pinpointed the apparent focal point of the phenomenon you can begin to try to make contact with the ghost or, to put it another way, tune into the psi field at that spot. If the ghost is a noisy one—that is, a poltergeist—try establishing a code and asking it questions, treating it for the time being as a living entity in the same way you did the glass and table. You can ask it to signify "yes" by two taps, "no" by one. If the ghost is a silent one, use the table, glass, Ouija board or pendulum as a means of communication.

Signs of apparent intelligence produced spontaneously or as a result of such inquiry, combined with the fact that hauntings have sometimes been successfully defused as a result of such attempts at communication, tend to lend credence to the Unquiet Spirit hypothesis. Parapsychologists, however, tend to theorize that the defusing operation, when it does occur, is less an exorcism than a psychoanalytic airing of a repressed complex. In this instance, the knotty emotional problem has somehow outlived the death of its originator and become rooted to the place where he lived. Perhaps we can think of a haunting as a permanent emotional twist inflicted on the local psi field, which continues to emerge and express itself through the psi field of living individuals who come within range.

ELEVEN

Putting It All Together

In a book of this sort, it would be nice if one could tie up in one chapter all the fascinating fields we have discussed and even produce a neat little set of golden psi rules to live by. But how, in all honesty, can one—since the data of psi, real and evident though they may be, are still so fluid, so open to many interpretations?

About the best one can manage at present is to state that the fact of psi's existence indicates we are severely mistaken about the prosaic view we hold of our own lives. All the evidence garnered by today's parapsychologists suggests that not only are we more in touch with one another and the events in our lives than we generally realize but we are also more actively involved in influencing what goes on around us than we give ourselves credit for. How we feel and think about things important to us in our lives must, given the existence of ESP and PK, *alter* those things to some degree, maybe in a way similar to that in which a physicist's observation of an electron alters its very nature.

Because psi is real it falls within the scope of scientific inquiry. The riddles posed by paranormal phenomena undoubtedly are based on the complexities of a physics of some sort; a physics beyond the bounds of our present knowledge, but physics nonetheless. Because a phenomenon is elusive does not mean it is irrational. What principles are involved, and the manner of their involvement, have yet to be determined.

This, of course, is only the narrow view of psi. What of the broad, speculative one?

Psi may one day offer us a key to the solution of a great many of man's problems. If people really came to understand and *experience* the facts of ESP—namely, that in consciousness, at least, we are all part of one another—the brotherhood of man would become something more than just an idealistic goal to pay lip service to. Could it be, one wonders, that the discovery of psi at *this* point in our history represents the beginning of a new sweep of the evolutionary curve for man? Perhaps the discovery of radio and atomic energy, gigantic leaps forward though they were, were only precursors of a far more radical change in our own beings in the not-too-distant future? This change may well be ushered in by the meeting and melding of two presently divergent disciplines: physics and psychology. Could we already be witnessing the inception of this science of "psychophysics" in the newly developed techniques of biofeedback? Such a science will not come of age, however, until the facts of psi can be accounted for within its framework, at which point parapsychology may well cease to exist as a separate discipline. Controlled psi may one day offer us a key to the solution of matters presently beyond the limits of our comprehension: the riddles of time and causality itself. In a world where space and time are running short all too fast, such a possibility, tenuous though it may seem to the unimaginative, is surely an appealing one.

But what can all this mean to us personally? Such possibilities may be fine for future generations, but what can psi offer us here and now in relation to our own search for meaning and fulfillment? What of that ever-present awareness of the certainty of our own deaths? Can psi offer any light to illuminate that darkness?

A hope, yes, undoubtedly; but not a guarantee. Even as birth may not be the beginning of it all, so death may not be its end. Consciousness may still be a mystery, but it is a fact. Conservation of energy seems to be a cornerstone of reality, and what is consciousness if not a type of energy? Even if we choose to discount the evidence for reincarnation memories, for Cross Correspondences among mediums and even for the repeated experience of out-of-the-body states, our view of death must be changed by ESP itself, for its occurrence indicates that man's consciousness is a public phenomenon, not a private one. We are all inextricably joined to one another, if we are not indeed part of one another. While one man lives on earth, in this sense we cannot die. But the continuity of personal consciousness? That has yet to be ascertained. Maybe we shall have some answers soon. That is, provided we continue to ask the questions.

Appendixes

APPENDIX 1

Progressive Relaxation Exercises

Progressive Relaxation is a technique evolved during the 1930's by Edmund Jacobson, a research worker in clinical physiology from Chicago. As an extremely simple but very effective means of inducing total muscular relaxation, it can be used in any type of psi experiment that requires this condition (such as ESP or OBE training).

The object of the method, which is in effect an exercise in feedback learning, is to teach the practitioner the *feeling* of total relaxation in all his muscle groups in order that he may learn to switch the state on and off at will.

The initial exercises can take up to ten minutes to run through, but after the technique has been learned, they can be abbreviated to three minutes and finally to around twenty seconds.

To begin, seat yourself in a comfortable armchair or lie flat on the floor or on a bed. Each of your chief groups of muscles is going to be successively tensed then relaxed several times for between two and five seconds, in the following order:

Group 1. Clench the fist of your dominant hand (the hand you write with) tightly for five seconds. Now relax it for five seconds. Repeat three times.

Group 2. Now tense the biceps of this arm for five seconds. Again relax for five seconds. Repeat three times.

Group 3. Now clench and relax your other fist for the same amount of time, three times.

Group 4. Tense the biceps of this arm in the same way, and relax three times.

Group 5. Now either raise your eyebrows hard, or frown hard, thus tensing the muscles in your forehead for five seconds. Relax for five seconds. Repeat three times.

Group 6. Wrinkle your nose hard, tensing the muscles in your nose and upper cheeks for five seconds. Relax for five seconds. Repeat three times.

Group 7. Now pull back the corners of your mouth to tense the muscles in your lower cheeks and jaws for five seconds. Then relax for five seconds. Repeat three times.

Group 8. Now pull your chin down to your chest, but prevent it from touching by tensing your neck muscles. Do this for five seconds, then relax for five seconds. Repeat three times.

Group 9. Take a deep breath, hold it and pull your shoulder blades back. Hold for five seconds. Then let the breath out and relax for five seconds. Repeat three times.

Group 10. Now tense your stomach muscles as though you were about to receive a punch there. Hold for five seconds. Relax for five seconds. Repeat three times.

Group 11. Now tense the upper thigh of the leg on the same side of your body as your dominant hand for five seconds. Relax for five seconds. Repeat three times.

Group 12. Now make the foot of that leg assume a right angle to the shin by pulling the toes up and producing tension in the calf. Hold for five seconds, then relax. Repeat three times.

Group 13. Point the toes of that foot and curl them *gently* inward for two seconds—you don't want to cause a cramp. Relax and repeat three times.

Group 14. Now tense the upper thigh of the opposite leg for five seconds. Relax for five seconds. Repeat three times.

Group 15. Now tense the muscle in the calf for five seconds. Relax. Repeat three times.

Group 16. Point the toes and curl them gently for a couple of seconds. Relax and repeat three times.

This completes your first series of exercises. Once you have learned how to make your muscles do what you want and got the *feel* of the state of relaxation that follows the tension—this is the important point—you can start abbreviating. Instead of tensing the muscles of the hand, forearm and biceps separately, combine the action by tensing all three at once. We can reduce our original sixteen muscle groups to seven, as follows:

Group 1. Dominant arm. (Original groups 1 and 2.)

Group 2. Alternate arm. (Original groups 3 and 4.)

Group 3. Face. (Original groups 5, 6 and 7.)

Group 4. Neck and throat. (Original group 8.)

Group 5. Torso. (Original groups 9 and 10.)

Group 6. Dominant leg. (Original groups 11, 12 and 13.)

Group 7. Alternate leg. (Original groups 14, 15 and 16.)

This reduction will cut your exercise time down to about two or three minutes. Once you have mastered it—making yourself especially aware of the *feeling* of the relaxation, remember—you can abbreviate it further into four muscle groups as follows:

Group 1. Both arms. (Original groups 1, 2, 3 and 4.)

Group 2. Head. (Original groups 5, 6, 7 and 8.)

Group 3. Torso. (Original groups 9 and 10.)

Group 4. Both legs. (Original groups 11, 12, 13, 14, 15 and 16.)

Now try the exercise while counting to yourself from one to ten. Count on each out-breath you make. On "one" and "two," tense and relax muscle group 1. On "three" and "four," tense and relax group 2. On "five" and "six," tense and relax group 3. On "seven" and "eight," tense and relax group 4. On "nine" and "ten," be aware of the feeling of total relaxation throughout your body.

Once you have tried this, you can proceed to the final stage: switching on your relaxation *without* doing any tensing exercises first, for you will by now have taught your muscles the correct feeling of relaxation. As you count from one to ten, simply let your muscles relax in the way they have learned. At "ten" you will have attained a state of practically complete muscular relaxation in from ten to twenty seconds.

APPENDIX 2

Notes and References in the Text

CHAPTER TWO   *Understanding ESP*

1. R. A. McConnell, *ESP Curriculum Guide* (New York: Simon and Schuster, 1971), p. 63.
2. Robert L. Morris, "Psi and Animal Behavior: A Survey," *Journal of the American Society for Psychical Research* (hereafter referred to as *J. ASPR*), LXIV (July, 1970), 242–260.
3. See A. Hardy, "Biology and ESP," in J. R. Smythies, ed., *Science and ESP* (London: Routledge and Kegan Paul, 1967).
4. Lyndon Rose and Ronald Rose, "Psi Experiments with Australian Aborigines," *Journal of Parapsychology*, XV (1951), 122–131.
5. See R. G. Stanford, "An Experimentally Testable Model for Spontaneous Psi Events," *J. ASPR*, LXVIII (January, 1974).
6. See L. J. Ravitz, "Electromagnetic Field Monitoring of Changing State-Function, Including Hypnotic States," *Journal of the American Society of Psychosomatic Dentistry and Medicine*, XVII (1970), 119–129.
7. L. L. Vasiliev, *Experiments in Mental Suggestion*, trans. from Russian (Church Crookham Hunts, England: Galley Hill Press, I.S.M.I. Publications, 1963). For a possible refutation also see H. Margenau on quantum tunnel effects in "ESP in the Framework of Modern Science," in J. R. Smythies, ed., *Science and ESP* (London: Routledge and Kegan Paul, 1967), p. 220.
8. With regard to psi fields, see J. G. Pratt, "A Decade of Research with a Selected ESP Subject: An Overview and Reappraisal of the Work with Pavel Stepanek," *Proceedings of the ASPR*, XXX (September, 1973). Also W. G. Roll, "The Psi Field," *Proceedings of the Parapsychological Association*, I (1957–1964), 32–65.

9. See J. B. Rhine, *The Reach of the Mind* (New York: William Sloane, 1947), pp. 32–36.

10. Pratt, "A Decade of Research with a Selected ESP Subject: An Overview and Reappraisal of the Work with Pavel Stepanek."

11. For speculations pro and con time reversal, see H. Reichenbach, *The Direction of Time* (California: University of California Press, 1956); H. Margenau, "Can Time Flow Backwards?" *Philosophy of Science*, XXI (1954), 79–92; J. V. Narlikar, "Neutrinos and the Arrow of Time," *Proceedings of the Royal Society*, London Series A (1962), 553–563.

12. Rhine, *The Reach of the Mind*, pp. 65–85.

13. See G. N. M. Tyrrell, *Science and Psychical Phenomena* (London: Methuen, 1938).

14. S. Krippner, M. Ullman and C. Honorton, "A Precognitive Dream Study with a Single Subject," *J. ASPR*, LXV (April, 1971).

15. For a good résumé of some of these theories, see A. Koestler, *The Roots of Coincidence* (New York: Random House, 1972); also Smythies, *Science and ESP*.

16. C. W. K. Mundle, "The Explanation of ESP," in Smythies, *Science and ESP*.

17. See M. Ruderfer, "Note on the Effect of Distance on ESP," *J. ASPR*, LXIII (April, 1969); also M. Ruderfer, "Letter to the Editor," *J. ASPR*, LXII (January, 1968). For the originator of the ESP neutrino theory, see A. L. Hammond, "A Note on Telepathic Communication," *Proceedings of the Institute of Radio Engineers* XL (1952), 605.

18. See K. Osis, "ESP over a Distance," *J. ASPR*, LIX (January, 1965); and M. E. Turner, Jr., "A Statistical Model for Examining the Relationship Between ESP and Distance," *J. ASPR*, LIX (January, 1965). See also A. Dobbs, "The Feasibility of a Physical Theory of ESP," in Smythies, *Science and ESP*, pp. 225–254.

19. For details of Edgar D. Mitchell and Olof Jonsson's ESP test between Apollo 14 and Earth, see *Journal of Parapsychology*, XXXV (June 1971).

20. See J. Ehrenwald, *Telepathy and Medical Psychology* (New York: Norton, 1948); J. Eisenbud, *Psi and Psychoanalysis* (New York: Grune and Stratton, 1970); E. Servadio, "Telepathy and Psychoanalysis," *J. ASPR*, LII (1958). For an overview of the field of psi and psychoanalysis see also E. Servadio, "Psychoanalysis and Parapsychology," in Smythies, *Science and ESP*, pp. 255–261.

21. C. G. Jung and W. Pauli, *The Interpretation of Nature and the Psyche* (London: Routledge and Kegan Paul, 1955), p. 14.

22. See Stanford, "An Experimentally Testable Model for Spontaneous Psi Events."

CHAPTER THREE *Demonstrating ESP for Yourself*

1. W. Carington, *Thought Transference: An Outline of Facts, Theory and Implications of Telepathy* (New York: Creative Age Press, 1946).
2. R. Warcollier, *Mind to Mind* (New York: Collier Books, 1963); U. Sinclair, *Mental Radio* (Springfield, Illinois: Charles C. Thomas, 1930, 1962).
3. Warcollier, *Mind to Mind.*
4. See C. E. Stuart, "Personality Measurements and ESP Tests with Cards and Drawings," *Journal of Parapsychology*, XI (1947), 118-146.
5. See L. E. Rhine, *Mind over Matter* (New York: Collier Books, 1970), pp. 21-25; also J. B. Rhine and J. G. Pratt, *Parapsychology* (Springfield, Illinois: Charles C. Thomas, 1957). (Also see Glossary under CR.)
6. See J. G. Pratt, "Some Notes for the Future Einstein for Parapsychology," *J. ASPR*, LXVIII (April, 1974), 146-155.
7. See B. K. Kanthamani and K. R. Rao, "Personality Characteristics of ESP Subjects": II. "The Combined Personality Measure (CPM) and ESP," *Journal of Parapsychology*, XXXVI (1972), 56-70.
8. See M. Ullman, "The Experimentally Induced Telepathic Dream: Theoretical Implications," *J. ASPR*, LXIV (October, 1970), 358-374; M. Ullman and S. Krippner, *Dream Studies and Telepathy: An Experimental Approach*, Parapsychological Monographs No. 12 (New York: Parapsychological Foundation, 1970); C. Honorton, "Significant Factors in Hypnotically Induced Clairvoyant Dreams," *J. ASPR*, LXVI (January, 1972), 86-102; Krippner, Ullman, Honorton, "A Precognitive Dream Study."
9. Central Premonitions Registry, Box 482, Times Square Station, New York, New York 10036.
10. See C. Green, *Lucid Dreams* (London: Hamish Hamilton, 1968). See also C. McCreery, *Psychical Phenomena and the Physical World* (New York: Ballantine, 1973), pp. 3-28, 105-134.

CHAPTER FOUR *Developing Your ESP*

1. R. G. Stanford and C. Lovin, "EEG Alpha Activity and ESP Performance," *J. ASPR*, LXIV (October, 1970), 375-384. Also R. G. Stanford, "EEG Alpha Activity and ESP Performance: A Replicative Study," *J. ASPR*, LXV (April, 1971), 144-154.
2. For an engrossing account of the "Cross Correspondences" see

Rosalind Heywood, *The Sixth Sense* (London: Pan Books, 1966), pp. 69–92. For an attempted recent replication of the experiment see also K. Osis, "Linkage Experiments with Mediums," *J. ASPR*, LX (April, 1966).

3. E. D. Dean, "Plethysmograph Recordings as ESP Responses," *International Journal of Neuropsychiatry*, II (October, 1966).

4. For material on dowsing see S. Tromp, "Review of Possible Physiological Causes of Dowsing," *International Journal of Parapsychology*, X (1968). See also Joseph Baum, *The Beginner's Handbook of Dowsing* (New York: Crown, 1974).

5. M. Ryzl, *How to Develop ESP in Yourself and Others* (privately printed: Dr. Milan Ryzl, Box 9459, Westgate Station, San Jose, California).

6. J. Trithemius, *Steganographia*, quoted in D. P. Walker, *Spiritual and Demonic Magic from Ficino to Campanella* (London: Warburg Institute, University of London, 1958), pp. 87–88. See also L. Thorndike, *A History of Magic and Experimental Science* (New York and London: Columbia University Press, 1966), IV, p. 525.

7. H. C. Agrippa, "De Occulta Philosophia," I, vi, in D. P. Walker, *Spiritual and Demonic Magic*, p. 88.

8. See Gershom G. Scholem, *Major Trends in Jewish Mysticism* (New York: Schocken Books, 1961), pp. 119–155. Also T. Schrive, *Hebrew Amulets* (London: Routledge and Kegan Paul, 1966).

9. See note 14, Chapter Two.

10. B. Steiger, *The Psychic Feats of Olaf Jonsson* (Englewood Cliffs, N.J.: Prentice-Hall, 1971), p. 84.

11. See E. Garrett, *Telepathy: In Search of a Lost Faculty* (New York: Creative Age Press, 1945), pp. 9–13 and 35–39.

CHAPTER FIVE   *Using Your ESP*

1. See G. R. Schmeidler and R. A. McConnell, *ESP and Personality Patterns* (New Haven: Yale University Press, 1958).

2. Garrett, *Telepathy*, pp. 43–44.

3. See J. C. Carpenter, "The Differential Effect and Hidden Target Differences Consisting of Erotic and Neutral Stimuli," *J. ASPR*, LXV (April, 1971), 204–214. See also G. W. Fisk and D. J. West, "ESP Tests with Erotic Symbols," *Journal of the Society for Psychical Research*, XXXVIII (March, 1955), 1–7; (September, 1955), 134–136.

4. R. A. White, "A Comparison of Old and New Methods of Response to Targets in ESP Experiments," *J. ASPR*, LVIII (January, 1964), 21–56.

5. Garrett, *Telepathy*, p. 51.

6. *Ibid.*

7. *Ibid.*, p. 151.

8. *Ibid.*, p. 51.
9. *Ibid.*, p. 175.
10. A good review of some of the findings of experimental psychometry can be found in W. G. Roll, "Pagenstecher's Contribution to Parapsychology," *J. ASPR*, LXI (July, 1967), 219–240. See also the discussion of the ESP Focusing Effect in Pratt, "A Decade of Research with a Selected ESP Subject."
11. Roll, "Pagenstecher's Contribution to Parapsychology."
12. Garrett, *Telepathy*, p. 156.

CHAPTER SIX   *Tracking Down Past Incarnations*

1. I. Stevenson, "Twenty Cases Suggestive of Reincarnation," *Proceedings of the American Society for Psychical Research*, XXVI (September, 1966).
2. *Ibid.*, pp. 134–150.
3. W. F. Prince, *The Case of Patience Worth* (Boston: Boston Society for Psychical Research, 1927). For reports on a recent extraordinary case, see also I. Stevenson, "Xenoglossy: A Review and Report of a Case," *Proceedings of the ASPR*, XXXI (February, 1974).

CHAPTER SEVEN   *The Out-of-the-Body Experience*

1. Originally written OOBE, OBE has now been adopted (as of April, 1974) by the ASPR, at the suggestion of John Beloff of Edinburgh University, as a less unwieldy abbreviation.
2. A recent and concise breakdown of the salient features of OBE's was made by Celia Green in *Out-of-the-Body Experiences* (New York: Ballantine, 1973). See also McCreery, *Psychical Phenomena and the Physical World*, pp. 29–45, 159–170.
3. Professor C. D. Broad discusses the logical approach to these speculations in his lecture on "Dreams and Out-of-the-Body Experiences," in *"Lectures on Psychical Research,"* ed. Ted Honderich, *International Library of Philosophy and Scientific Method* (London: Routledge and Kegan Paul, 1966), pp. 153–189.
4. E. Gurney, F. Myers and F. Podmore, *Phantasms of the Living* (London: Trubner, 1886).
5. *ASPR Newsletters* nos. 14 and 18; ASPR, 5 West 73rd Street, New York, New York 10023. See also C. T. Tart, "A Psychophysiological Study of Out-of-the-Body Experiences in a Selected Subject," *J. ASPR*, LXII (January, 1968), 3–27.
6. E. A. de Rochas, *L'Extériorisation de la Sensibilité* (Paris, 1895).
7. H. M. Durville, *Le Fantôme des Vivants* (Paris, 1909).
8. C. Lancelin, *Méthodes de Dédoublement Personnel,* summarized in

Hereward Carrington, *Higher Psychical Phenomena* (London: Kegan Paul, Trench Trubner, 1920).

9. *J. ASPR*, X (1916), 632–61, 679–708.
10. *J. ASPR*, XII (1918), 36–60.
11. Carrington, *Higher Psychical Phenomena*.
12. S. J. Muldoon and H. Carrington, *The Projection of the Astral Body* (London: Rider, 1929; reprinted New York: Samuel Weiser, 1970).
13. O. Fox, "The Pineal Door," *The Occult Review* (1920), 256–264, 317–327. See also O. Fox, *A Record of Out-of-the-Body Experiences* (New York: University Books, 1962).
14. R. A. Monroe, *Journeys Out of the Body* (New York: Doubleday, Anchor, 1973).
15. *J. ASPR*, X (1916), 643, 649, 680–681, 706.
16. Muldoon and Carrington, *The Projection of the Astral Body*, pp. 151–152, 227–230.
17. D. Scott Rogo has written interestingly of positive results he obtained by following the Keeler diet in "Astral Projection: A Risky Practice?" *Fate* magazine, XXVI (May, 1973), 74–80.
18. Lancelin, *Méthodes de Dédoublement*, in Carrington, *Higher Psychical Phenomena*.
19. Monroe, *Journeys Out of the Body*, p. 211.
20. J. ASPR, X (1916), 649.
21. See Appendix I.
22. A. E. Moriarty and G. Murphy, "Some Thoughts About Prerequisite Conditions or States in Creativity and Paranormal Experience," *J. ASPR*, LXI (July, 1967), 210.
23. See M. Eliade, *Shamanism: Archaic Techniques of Ecstasy* (New York: Bollingen, 1964).
24. *Ibid.*, p. 260.
25. Ophiel, *The Art and Practice of Astral Projection* (San Francisco: Peach Publishing Co., 1962), pp. 26–33.
26. *Ibid.*, p. 28.
27. Monroe, *Journeys Out of the Body*, pp. 203–227.
28. Write to:
    Director of Research
    American Society for Psychical Research
    5 West 73rd Street
    New York, New York 10023
        or
    Survival Research Coordinator
    Psychical Research Foundation
    Duke Station
    Durham, North Carolina 27706

CHAPTER EIGHT   *Psychokinesis—Mind over Matter?*

1. L. E. Rhine, *Mind over Matter: Psychokinesis* (New York: Collier Books, 1972).
2. *Ibid.*, pp. 251–290.
3. H. Schmidt, "Comparison of PK Action on Two Different Random Number Generators," *Journal of Parapsychology*, XXXVIII (March, 1974), 47–55. See also H. Schmidt, "A Quantum Process in Psi Testing," in J. B. Rhine, ed., *Progress in Parapsychology* (Durham, North Carolina: Parapsychology Press), pp. 28–35.
4. Schmidt, "Comparison of PK Action."
5. Report in Rome *Tribuna*, March 5, 1905, quoted in N. Fodor, *Encyclopedia of Psychic Science* (New York: University Books, 1966), p. 292.
6. W. G. Roll, *The Poltergeist* (New York: Signet, 1972), pp. 91–93; A. Hardy, R. Harvie and A. Koestler, *The Challenge of Chance* (New York: Random House, 1973), pp. 195–200; H. Bender, "An Investigation of 'Poltergeist' Occurrences," *Proceedings of the Parapsychological Association*, no. 5 (1968), pp. 31–33; H. Bender, "New Developments in Poltergeist Research," *Proceedings of the Parapsychological Association*, no. 6 (1969), pp. 81–102.
7. J. Burton, *Heyday of a Wizard* (London: Harrap, 1948), p. 33.
8. E. Fielding, *Sittings with Eusapia Palladino* (New York: University Books, 1963), p. 27.
9. J. G. Pratt and H. H. J. Keil, "Firsthand Observations of Nina S. Kulagina Suggestive of PK upon Static Objects," *J. ASPR*, LXVII (October, 1973), 381–390.
10. See "Text of Stanford Research Institute Film" in A. Puharich, *Uri* (New York: Doubleday Anchor, 1974), pp. 263–271.
11. Roll, *The Poltergeist*, p. 150.
12. F. Bacon, *Sylva Sylvarum*, quoted in M. Bell, "Francis Bacon, Pioneer in Parapsychology," *International Journal of Parapsychology* VI (Spring, 1964), 199–208.
13. R. G. Stanford, "Associative Activation of the Unconscious and 'Visualization' as Methods for Influencing the PK Target," *J. ASPR*, LXIII (October, 1969), 338–351.
14. L. E. Rhine, *Mind over Matter*, p. 177.
15. B. Grad, "A Telekinetic Effect on Plant Growth," *International Journal of Parapsychology*, V (1963), 117–133; VI (1964), 473–498.
16. B. Grad, "The Laying on of Hands: Implications for Psychotherapy, Gentling, and the Placebo Effect," *J. ASPR*, LXI (1967), 286–305.

CHAPTER NINE   *Using PK in Daily Life*

1. If factual, the incident of Jesus's healing the woman with a

hemorrhage mentioned in Mark 5:25–34 could presumably be an instance of this type of healing.

2. R. Feldman and S. Yamamoto, "Massage in Oriental Medicine: Its Development and Relationship to 'Ki' or Vital Energy," in S. Krippner and D. Rubin, eds., *The Kirlian Aura* (New York: Doubleday Anchor, 1974), p. 154.
3. See Harry Edwards, *The Healing Intelligence* (New York: Taplinger, 1971), pp. 104–112.
4. Feldman and Yamamoto, "Massage in Oriental Medicine," in Krippner and Rubin, *The Kirlian Aura*, pp. 154–155.
5. Garrett, *Telepathy*, pp. 100–105.
6. An interesting personal exploration of paranormal healing, often overlooked by parapsychologists because of its radiesthesia affiliations, is L. E. Eeman, *Co-operative Healing: The Curative Properties of Human Radiations* (London: Frederick Muller, 1947).

CHAPTER TEN   *On Seeing Ghosts*

1. See G. N. M. Tyrrell, *Apparitions* (New York: Collier Books, 1963). See also Broad, *Lectures on Psychical Research*, pp. 113–152. See also McCreery, *Psychical Phenomena*, pp. 47–63.
2. For the full version of the PRF Questionnaire, see *Theta* magazine, no. 16 (Winter, 1967), Duke Station, Durham, North Carolina 27706.
3. G. R. Schmeidler, "Quantitative Investigation of a 'Haunted House,'" *J. ASPR*, LX (April, 1966), 137–149.

APPENDIX 3

Glossary

ACAUSAL. Not related by normal cause-and-effect links.

AGENT. 1. The "sender" in ESP tests. 2. The person whose PK is responsible for poltergeist phenomena.

ALPHA. Electrical pulse of 8 to 13 cycles per second generated by the human brain, generally associated with a relaxed, yet alert, mental state.

ANPSI. Animal psi.

ASC. Altered state of consciousness.

ASSOCIATION. Mental process of linking perceptions, feelings, ideas or images.

AUTOGENIC TRAINING. A technique of regulating certain body functions by self-hypnosis.

AUTOMATISM. An unconscious action, sometimes performed in a state of trance.

AUTOSUGGESTION. Modifying one's behavior by giving oneself verbalized or visualized suggestions. *(See* SUGGESTION.*)*

BETA. Electrical pulse of 13 to 26 cycles per second generated by the human brain, generally associated with problem solving, concentration and anxiety. Roll suggests that poltergeist phenomena are associated with the beta state of the agent.

BIOENERGY. Soviet term with approximately the same meaning as psychokinesis. *(See* PK.*)*

BIOFEEDBACK. Learning to control previously uncontrollable body processes and mental states by using an electronic device to monitor them and provide one with feedback. The EEG, EKG, GSR and EMG (qq.v.) can be used as biofeedback devices.

BIOLOGICAL INFORMATION. Soviet term corresponding to ESP (q.v.).

BIOPLASMA. Soviet term for Psi Field (q.v.).

BT: BASIC TECHNIQUE. J. B. Rhine's card clairvoyance test in which each card is laid aside by the experimenter as it is called by the subject. The checkup is made at the end of the run.

CALL. The subject's guess in trying to identify the target in an ESP test.

CHANCE: MEAN CHANCE EXPECTATION, CHANCE EXPECTATION, CHANCE AVERAGE. The most likely score in an ESP or PK test if only chance is involved.

CHI SQUARE. A statistical term meaning a sum of quantities, each of which is a derivation squared, divided by an expected value. A sum of the CR's squared. (*See* CR.)

CLAIRVOYANCE. 1. Traditional meaning: second sight; sixth sense. 2. Parapsychological definition: extrasensory perception of objects or objective events.

CLOSED PACK. Pack of ESP Cards (q.v.) composed of five each of five symbols.

CPM. Combined Personality Measure. A scale used for psychological evaluation.

CR. Critical Ratio. A measure to determine whether the observed deviation in a psi test is significantly greater than the expected fluctuation around chance. The CR is obtained by dividing the observed deviation by the standard deviation. The observed deviation is the number of hits minus the expected chance average of hits. In tests using ESP Cards the standard deviation is the square root of the number of runs multiplied by two. The resulting CR is looked up in statistical tables to check the probability of its occurring. The smaller the probability number, the more indicative it becomes that ESP has occurred.

DECLINE EFFECT. Generally observed tendency for scoring rate to drop off toward the end of psi tests.

DELTA. Electrical pulses produced by the human brain that measure between 0.5 to 4 cycles per second; generally associated with states of unconsciousness and deep dreamless sleep.

DEVIATION. The amount an observed number of successes in a psi test varies, either above or below mean chance expectation of a run, series or other unit of trials.

DISPLACEMENT. ESP responses to targets preceding or following those for which the calls were intended.

DISSOCIATION. Term describing a mental state of abstraction from the outer world, ranging in scope from light reverie to deep sleep, mediumistic trance or hypnosis.

DOUBLE-BLIND. A psi test in which both the subject and the experimenter are kept ignorant of the target material or effect being tested.

DT: DOWN THROUGH: Rhine's clairvoyance test in which the cards are called down through the deck before any are removed or checked.

ECSOMATIC. Out-of-the-body.

EEG. Electroencephalograph: Machine that electronically measures brain currents.

EKG, ECG. Electrocardiograph: Machine that electronically measures the heartbeat.

ELECTROENCEPHALOGRAPH. *See* EEG.

EMG. Electromyograph: Machine that electronically measures muscle tension.

ESP. EXTRASENSORY PERCEPTION. A psychophysical response to an unknown event not presented to any known sense. ESP includes Telepathy, Clairvoyance, Precognition and Retrocognition (qq.v.).

ESP CARDS. Pack of twenty-five cards used in ESP testing containing five each of the following symbols: star, circle, cross, square, wavy lines. *(See* Closed Pack, Open Pack.)

EXTRACHANCE: Not due to chance alone.

FARADAY CAGE. A room electrically shielded from electromagnetic radiation.

FOCUSING EFFECT. Observed tendency among ESP sensitives and PK agents to zero in on certain targets in preference to others.

FORCED CHOICE. An ESP test with a specified and limited number of targets to choose from. Opposite of Free Material (q.v.).

FREE ASSOCIATION. Free-flowing, unselected chain of mental associations.

FREE MATERIAL. Target objects in an ESP test in which the range of possible targets is unspecified.

GESP. GENERAL ESP. Either Telepathy or Clairvoyance (qq.v.) or both.

GLOBAL. An image, perception or process that is very primitive and highly undifferentiated.

"GOAT." Gertrude Schmeidler's term for a person resistant to the concept of ESP. Opposite of "Sheep" (q.v.).

GSR: GALVANIC SKIN RESPONSE. Device that measures changes in electrical skin resistance in response to an outside stimulus.

HYPNOSIS. An induced and sometimes sleeplike state of suggestibility accompanied by a narrowing of the range of attention.

IMPRESSION. Vague mental experience, image, judgment or feeling —possibly mediated by psi.

INTROSPECTION. Deliberate focusing of the attention inward upon subjective ideas, feelings, visions, sounds or impressions.

KIRLIAN PHOTOGRAPHY. Controversial technique of electrostatic photography invented by Soviet technician Semyon Kirlian. Observable changes in the corona of sparks displayed around an object placed in a high frequency electrical field are alleged by Kirlian and his followers to reflect changes in its bioplasma (q.v.) field too.

LATENCY. René Warcollier's term for the observed time lag between the transmission and perception of a psi signal.

LUCID DREAM. Dream in which the subject realizes he is dreaming.

OBE, OOBE: OUT-OF-THE-BODY EXPERIENCE. "Astral projection." Experience of seeming to be outside one's physical body.

OPEN PACK. An ESP pack of twenty-five cards but containing no fixed number of each symbol. (*See* Closed Pack.)

OUT-OF-THE-BODY EXPERIENCE. *See* OBE.

PARANORMAL. Attributable to psi.

PARAPSYCHOLOGY. The branch of science that deals with psi. Term adapted by by J. B. Rhine during the 1920's from the French psychologist Emil Boirac's *parapsychique,* implying "beyond psychology." It was ratified for general use among psychic researchers at the 1953 International Conference of Psychical Research at Utrecht, Holland.

PERCIPIENT. The person experiencing ESP; also one who is tested for ESP ability. Opposite of Agent (q.v.).

PK: PSYCHOKINESIS. J. B. Rhine's term for the extramotor aspect of psi; an apparently direct (that is, mental but nonmuscular) influence exerted by the subject on an external physical process, condition or object.

PLACEMENT TEST. Haakon Forwald's PK technique in which the aim of the subject is to try to influence falling objects (such as dice) to come to rest in a designated area of the throwing surface.

PLETHYSMOGRAPH. Biofeedback device used to measure fluctuations in blood pressure.

PRECOGNITION. Noninferential awareness of, or reaction to, future events that cannot be deduced from normally known data in the present.

PROGRESSIVE RELAXATION. Technique of muscular relaxation devised by Edmund Jacobson in 1934.

PSI. Thouless and Wiesner's term to identify general extrasensorimotor exchange with the environment. Psi includes ESP and PK (qq.v.).

PSI DIFFERENTIAL EFFECT. Significant difference between scoring rates when subjects are participating in an experiment in which two procedural conditions (such as two different targets or guessing methods) are compared.

PSI FIELD. W. G. Roll's hypothesis of an as yet undetected field of psychic force surrounding physical objects responsible for ESP and PK phenomena. The strength of the field is reduced with increased distance from the source. When psi energy is transformed to other energy forms (e.g., kinetic) the total energy is conserved.

PSI HITTING, PSI MISSING. Psi exercised in a way that causes the subject either to hit or to avoid hitting (missing) the target.

PSI PHENOMENA. Occurrences that result from the operation of psi. E.g., ESP, PK, poltergeists, ghosts, etc.

PSYCHIC. Sensitive (q.v.).

PSYCHICAL RESEARCH. Original term for parapsychology.

PSYCHOENERGETICS. Soviet term for Psi (q.v.).

PSYCHOKINESIS. *See* PK.

PSYCHOMETRY. Early term for the noninferential and paranormal acquisition of information by contact with an object associated with the said information.

PSYCHOPHYSIOLOGY. The physiology of mental processes.

PSYCHOSOMATIC. The influence of the mind over the body.

QD: QUARTER DISTRIBUTION. Analysis of psi tests by comparing the average rate of scoring down the run and across the page in the successive runs. Each run is divided into an upper and lower half, and the successive upper halves are divided into left and right parts, as are the two lower halves. The hits in the respective quarters are then totaled and compared to reveal any characteristic Decline Effects (*see* Decline Effect).

RANDOM ORDER. Chance arrangement.

RANDOMIZATION. Experimentally contrived chance choices or arrangements. Specially prepared Random Number Tables are often used by parapsychologists to effect randomization.

REM. Rapid Eye Movement, as observed in a person when he begins dreaming.

RETROCOGNITION. ESP of past events.

RSPK. Recurrent Spontaneous Psychokinesis: parapsychological explanation of poltergeist phenomena.

RUN. A standard group of trials in a psi test. In Rhine's ESP tests the run is usually twenty-five trials based on a pack of twenty-five ESP cards; in PK tests the standard run consists of twenty-four single die throws regardless of the number of dice thrown together.

SENSITIVE. Person with a pronounced or developed ESP ability.

"SHEEP." Gertrude Schmeidler's term for a person receptive to the concept of ESP. Opposite of "Goat" (q.v.).

SIGNIFICANT. A psi test is considered to show significant evidence of the action of psi when the numerical total of hits equals or surpasses some set standard of degree of chance improbability. The standard commonly used by today's parapsychologists is odds of 0.02 (50 to 1), or in stringent tests, 0.01 (100 to 1). Odds of 0.05 (20 to 1) are considered to be *suggestive* of psi activity but not indicative.

STIMULUS. Target (q.v.).

SUBJECT. The person tested in an experiment.

SUGGESTION. Alteration of a person's beliefs or state of consciousness by means of the spoken word.

SUGGESTIVE. *See* Significant.

TARGET. In ESP tests, the object or mental state to which the subject is trying to respond; in PK tests, the object or physical process that the subject is trying to influence.

TELEKINESIS. Early term for psychokinesis.

TELEPATHY. ESP of the mental state or activity of another person.

TRANCE. Early term for an altered state of consciousness characterized by unconsciousness or Dissociation (q.v.).

TRIAL. In ESP tests, a single attempt to identify a target (make a "hit"); in PK tests, a single unit of effect to be measured in the evaluation of results.

UNCONSCIOUS: UNCONSCIOUS MIND. All the hidden processes, memories and ideas latent in our mind of which we are not presently aware.

VERIDICAL. Myers's term meaning "corresponding to an external reality." It is still used to define true paranormal impressions.

XENOGLOSSY. Paranormal knowledge of foreign languages.

ZENER CARDS. ESP CARDS (q.v.).

APPENDIX 4

Bibliography

Baum, J. *The Beginner's Handbook of Dowsing*. New York: Crown, 1974.

Broad, C. D. *Lectures on Psychical Research*. London: Routledge and Kegan Paul, 1962.

Burton, J. *Heyday of a Wizard* (biography of D. D. Home). London: Harrap, 1948.

Carington, W. *Thought Transference*. New York: Creative Age Press, 1946.

Carrington, H. *Higher Psychical Phenomena*. London: Kegan, Paul, Trench Trubner, 1920.

Crookall, R. *The Techniques of Astral Projection*. London: Aquarian Press, 1964.

Dauven, J. *The Powers of Hypnosis*. New York: Stein and Day, 1971.

Ebon, M. (ed.). *Test Your ESP*. New York: Signet, 1971.

Edwards, H. *The Healing Intelligence*. New York: Taplinger, 1971.

Eeman, L. E. *Co-operative Healing*. London: Frederick Muller, 1947.

Ehrenwald, J. *Telepathy and Medical Psychology*. New York: Norton, 1948.

Eisenbud, J. *Psi and Psychoanalysis*. New York: Grune and Stratton, 1970.

Estabrooks, G. H. *Hypnotism*. New York: Dutton, 1957.

Fielding, E. *Sittings with Eusapia Palladino*. New York: University Books, 1966.

Fodor, N. *Encyclopedia of Psychic Science*. New York: University Books, 1966.

Fox, O. *A Record of Out-of-the-Body Experiences*. New York: University Books, 1962.

Fuller, G. *Biofeedback: A Research Bibliography*. 1973. Biofeedback Institute of San Francisco, 3428 Sacramento Street, San Francisco, California 94118.

Garrett, E. J. *Telepathy*. New York: Creative Age Press, 1945.

Green, C. *Lucid Dreams*. London: Hamish Hamilton, 1968.

———. *Out-of-the-Body Experiences*. New York: Ballantine, 1973.

Gurney, E., Myers, F., and Podmore, F. *Phantasms of the Living*. London: Trubner, 1886.

Hardy, A., Harvie, R., and Koestler, A. *The Challenge of Chance*. New York: Random House, 1973.

Heywood, R. *ESP: A Personal Memoir*. New York: Dutton, 1964.

———. *The Sixth Sense*. London: Pan, 1966. (U.S. title, *Beyond the Reach of Sense*.)

Jacobsen, E. *Progressive Relaxation*. Chicago: University of Chicago Press, 1938.

Jung, C. G. *Memories, Dreams, Reflections* (autobiography). New York: Pantheon, 1963.

———, and Pauli, W. *The Interpretation of Nature and the Psyche*. London: Routledge and Kegan Paul, 1955.

Koestler, A. *The Roots of Coincidence*. New York: Random House, 1972.

Krippner, S., and Rubin, D. (eds.). *The Kirlian Aura*. New York: Doubleday Anchor, 1974.

LeShan, L. *The Medium, the Mystic, and the Physicist*. New York: Viking, 1974.

McConnell, R. A. *ESP Curriculum Guide*. New York: Simon and Schuster, 1971.

McCreery, C. *Psychical Phenomena and the Physical World*. New York: Ballantine, 1973.

———. *Science, Philosophy and ESP*. London: Faber and Faber, 1967.

Mitchell, E., et al. *Psychic Exploration*. New York: G. P. Putnam, 1974.

Monroe, R. A. *Journeys Out of the Body*. New York: Doubleday Anchor, 1973.

Muldoon, S. J., and Carrington, H. *The Projection of the Astral Body*. New York: Weiser, 1970.

M phy, G., and Ballou, R. O. (eds.). *William James on Psychical Research*. London: Chatto and Windus, 1961.

, and Dale, L. *The Challenge of Psychical Research*. New York: Harper and Row, 1961.

Myers, F. W. H. *Human Personality and Its Survival of Bodily Death*, 2 vols. New York: Longmans Green, 1954.

Osis, K., and Turner, M. E., Jr. "Distance and ESP," *Proceedings of the ASPR*, XXVII (September, 1968).

Parapsychological Association. "Techniques and Status of Modern Parapsychology." First Symposium, 137th Annual Meeting of the American Association for the Advancement of Science, Chicago, Illinois, 1970.

Pratt, J. G. "A Decade of Research with a Selected ESP Subject: An

Overview and Reappraisal of the Work with Pavel Stepanek," *Proceedings of the ASPR,* XXX (September, 1973).

——, Rhine, J. B., et al. *Extrasensory Perception after Sixty Years.* Boston: Bruce Humphries, 1940.

Rao, K. R. *Experimental Parapsychology.* Springfield, Illinois: Charles C. Thomas, 1966.

Rhine, J. B. *Extrasensory Perception.* Boston: Bruce Humphries, 1935.

——. *The Reach of the Mind.* New York: Sloane, 1972.

—— (ed.). *Progress in Parapsychology.* 1973. Parapsychology Press, College Station, Box 6847, Durham, North Carolina 27708.

——, and Brier, R. (eds.). *Parapsychology Today.* New York: Citadel, 1968.

Rhine, L. E. *ESP in Life and Lab.* New York: Macmillan, 1967.

——. *Hidden Channels of the Mind.* New York: Sloane, 1961.

——. *Manual for Introductory Experiments in Parapsychology.* Institute for Parapsychology, College Station, Box 6847, Durham, North Carolina 27708.

——. *Mind over Matter: Psychokinesis.* New York: Collier Books, 1970.

Roll, W. G. *The Poltergeist.* New York: Signet, 1974.

Ryzl, M. *How to Develop ESP In Yourself and Others.* 1972. Milan Ryzl, Box 9459, Westgate Station, San Jose, California 95117.

Schmeidler, G. R., and McConnell, R. *ESP and Personality Patterns.* New Haven: Yale University Press, 1958.

Sinclair, U. *Mental Radio.* Springfield, Illinois: Charles C. Thomas, 1930, 1962.

Smythies, J. R. (ed.). *Science and ESP.* London: Routledge and Kegan Paul, 1967.

Soal, S. G., and Bateman, F. *Modern Experiments on Telepathy.* New Haven: Yale University Press, 1954.

Stevenson, I. "Telepathic Impressions," *Proceedings of the ASPR,* XXIX (June, 1970).

——. "Twenty Cases Suggestive of Reincarnation," *Proceedings of the ASPR,* XXVI (September, 1966).

——. "Xenoglossy: A Review and Report of a Case," *Proceedings of the ASPR,* XXXI (September, 1974).

Sudre, R. *Treatise on Parapsychology.* London: George Allen and Unwin, 1960.

Thouless, R. H. *Experimental Psychical Research.* London: Penguin, 1963.

——. *From Anecdote to Experiment in Psychical Research.* London: Routledge and Kegan Paul, 1972.

Tyrrell, G. N. M. *Apparitions.* New York: Collier Books, 1963.

———. *Science and Psychical Phenomena.* London: Methuen, 1938.

Vasiliev, L. L. *Experiments in Mental Suggestion* (trans. from Russian). Church Crookham, Hants, England: Galley Hill Press, I.S.M.I. Publications, 1963.

Warcollier, R. *Mind to Mind.* New York: Farrar, Straus, 1963.

White, R. A. "A Comparison of Old and New Methods of Response to Targets in ESP Experiments," *Journal of the ASPR,* LVIII (January, 1964).

———, and Dale, L. *Parapsychology: Sources of Information.* Scarecrow Press, P.O. Box 656, Metuchen, New Jersey 08840.

INDEX

reliability of, 150; research, 21, 179. *See also* Sensitive

Psychical Research Foundation (PRF), 24–25, 104, 105, 117

Psychoenergetics, 179. *See also* Psi

Psychokinesis (PK), 25, 118–40, 141–50, 154, 156, 173, 178; batteries, 144; broadcasting, 142; evaluation scale, 135; in daily life, 141; localized, 131, 139, 143–44; placement tests, 119, 179; plant experiments, 136; unconscious use of, 147

Psychometry, 27, 32, 92, 97, 144, 152, 171, 179. *See also* Object reading

Psychosomatic effect, 142, 179

QD (quarter distribution), 179

Quantum counter, 17, 119–20

Radioactive decay, effect of psi on, 120

Radionics, 144

Radio waves, 24

Randomization, 180

Random order, 180

Rao, K. R., 169

Rapid eye movement (REM), 105, 180

Rapid-fire guessing, 55

Rationales for psi, 20, 30, 69, 98, 107, 124, 136, 142

Rayleigh, Lord, 15

Recurrent spontaneous psychokinesis (RSPK), 123, 133, 180

Reichenbach, Karl von, 129

Reincarnation memories, 96–100, 161, 171

Relativity, theory of, 28, 128

Relaxation, importance of, 86, 87–88, 146. *See also* Progressive Relaxation

REM. *See* Rapid eye movement

Responsibility shifting, 74; by mediums, 69, 133; by healers, 146

Retrocognition, 32, 100, 180

Rhine, J. B., 12, 16, 21, 25, 26, 29, 31, 42, 50, 55, 118, 131, 136, 168, 176, 177, 178

Rhine, L. E., 169, 173

Richet, Charles, 21

Roll, William G., 24, 93, 126, 133, 167, 171, 173, 175, 179

Rosenheim poltergeist, 122, 128

RSPK. *See* Recurrent spontaneous psychokinesis

Run, 180

Ryzl, Milan, 75, 170

Sadducismus Triumphatus, Glanvill, 121

Scanning, ESP, 36, 37

Schizophrenia, 70, 111

Schmeidler, Gertrude R., 156, 170, 173, 177, 180

Schmidt, Helmut, 119, 173

Schultz, T. H., 109

Scrying, 81. *See also* Vision

Secondary personalities, 69, 97

Sensitive, 35, 180

Sergeev, G. A., 125

Shackleton, Basil, 13, 84

Shamanism, 68, 112, 172

"Sheep," 180

Significant scores, 51, 180. *See also* Tests, card guessing; Tests, dice throwing

Sinclair, Upton, 43, 169

Skepticism conducive to psi-missing, 56, 69, 73, 87

Smith, M. Justa, 145

Society for Psychical Research (SPR), 21, 26, 65, 106, 124

Somnambulism, 69

Soothsaying, 30

Soviet psychical research, 16, 24, 125, 176

Space, curvature of, 128

Spirit entities, 69, 102, 104, 124, 129; possession by, 69, 97, 133

Spiritual healing. *See* Psychic healing

Spiritualism, 68–69, 74, 124

SPR. *See* Society for Psychical Research

Standard ESP cards. *See* ESP, cards

Stanford, Rex G., 36, 40, 132, 133, 167, 169, 173

Static electricity, 131

Statistics, 34, 50; psi as a quirk of, 34, 119, 120

Stepanek, Pavel, 76, 167

Stevenson, Ian D., 96, 171

Sthenometer, 130

Stimulus. *See* Target

Subject, 180